Authentic Communication

Authentic Communication
Public Speaking for Everyone

Jeffrey Hannan, Travis Kiger, and Ganer Newman

International Debate Education Association

New York, Brussels & Amsterdam

Published by

International Debate Education Association
P.O. Box 922
New York, NY 10009

This book is published with the generous support of the Open Society
Foundations.

Library of Congress Cataloging-in-Publication Data

Hannan, Jeffrey.

  Authentic communication: public speaking for everyone / Jeffrey Hannan, Travis Kiger, and Ganer Newman.

    pages cm

  ISBN 978-1-61770-101-6

1. Public speaking. 2. Oratory--Study and teaching. 3. Oral communi-
cation--Study and teaching. 4. Oratory. 5. Speech acts (Linguistics) I.
Kiger, Travis. II. Newman, Ganer. III. International Debate Education
Association. IV. Title. V. Title: Public speaking for everyone.

  PN4086.H36 2015

  808.5'1--dc23

                        2015007392

Design by Kathleen Hayes

Printed in the USA

♥ IDEBATE Press

Contents

Preface.. xi

Chapter 1: Introduction to Public Speaking............................. 1
What Does It Mean to Speak in Public? 4
The Purposes of Public Speaking... 8
    Internal Purposes of Public Speaking.................................. 9
    External Purposes of Public Speaking 12
Tying It Together: Authentic Communication 13
Key Concepts 17

Chapter 2: Theory of Public Speaking.................................. 18
Ancient Times 19
The Classical Era 20
    The Greeks 20
    The Romans 26
Middle Ages and Renaissance 27
Modern Era 29
    Science.. 29
    Economics 30
    Media.. 31
Where Does That Leave Us 33
Tying It Together: Authentic Communication 35
Key Concepts 37

Chapter 3: Overcoming Communication Apprehension 38
Embrace the Nervous, Dispatch the Worry.................................. 39
    I'm Worried That I'll Pass Out....................................... 40

13/65/

How to Deal. 41

I'm Worried I'll Forget What to Say 42

How to Deal. 43

I'm Worried People Won't Understand What I Have to Say. 45

How to Deal. 45

I'm Worried People Won't Like What I Have to Say 47

How to Deal. 48

I'm Worried Another Speaker Will Be Better Than Me. 49

How to Deal. 49

Tying It Together: Authentic Communication 52

Key Concepts 54

Chapter 4: Writing for the Listening Audience. 55

Audiences Are Easily Distracted 56

Defining the Listening Audience 56

Structuring a Speech for the Listening Audience. 57

Adapting Your Writing for a Listening Audience. 59

Clear Writing. 59

Concise Writing 64

Coherent Writing. 66

A Note About Tone and Your Personal Voice 71

Tying It Together: Authentic Communication 72

Key Concepts 75

Chapter 5: Topic Selection 76

What Are We All Doing Here, Anyway?. 77

Why Am I Talking, Why Are You Listening?. 78

Speaking to Persuade 79

Speaking to Inform 80

A Storm is Coming—A BRAINstorm!. 81

We Need a Little Focus in Our Lives (and Speech Topics) 86

Writing a Great Thesis 86

Keep in Mind, You Can Always Change Yours. 87

Tying It Together: Authentic Communication 88

Key Concepts 91

Chapter 6: Research 93
Selecting a Topic Through Research 94
Why Research? 94
Sources 95
    But How Do I Find All These Sources? 97
    Conducting Interviews 100
What Do We Do With Research? 103
    Let's Organize This Piece 103
    Citing Sources 106
    How to Cite Sources 108
Tying It Together: Authentic Communication 110
Key Concepts 114

Chapter 7: Organization 115
Macro-Organization 115
    Undifferentiated Speech Organization 117
    Differentiated Speech Organization 121
      Informative Speaking 121
      Persuasive Speaking 123
    Handling Weak Points 126
Micro-Organization 127
    Previews 127
    Reviews 128
    Transitions 129
    Vehicles 134
Tying It Together: Authentic Communication 135
Key Concepts 137

Chapter 8: Introductions and Conclusions 138
Introduction to Introductions 139
Attention-getting Devices, or First Impressions Are Last Chances 139
Getting the Audience's Attention! 143
Include a Link 148
Justification 150
The Thesis 150

Conclusions 154

Tying It Together: Authentic Communication 157

Key Concepts 158

Chapter 9: Physical Delivery 159

Letting Your Body Do the Talking 160

Posture 160

Gestures 162

      Explanatory Gestures 164

      Expressive Gestures 167

      Using Space When Gesturing 169

      Using Stillness When Gesturing 172

Eye Contact 172

Move Your Face 174

Physical Delivery Using Limited Notes 176

Power Posing 178

Where to Stand 180

Walking 182

Tying It Together: Authentic Communication 183

Key Concepts 186

Chapter 10: Vocal Delivery 187

How Does Speaking Work? 187

      Why Planned Breathing is Important 188

      Don't Breathe With Your Chest 189

      Breathe With Your Diaphragm 189

      Good Vibrations 191

How to Speak Better 191

      Can the Audience Hear You? Thinking About Volume and Projection 192

      Thinking About Tempo and Pace 195

      Thinking About Articulation and Pronunciation 200

      Will the Audience Care? Thinking About Tone and Pitch 203

Tying It Together: Authentic Communication 205

Key Concepts 207

Chapter 11: Audience Analysis 209

What Makes Each Audience Unique 209

Frames of Reference 211
Learning About Your Audience 212
   Last-minute Audience Analysis 214
   Identifying a Target Audience 214
Applying Your Audience Analysis to Your Performance 215
   Adapting Content. 215
   Adapting Form 217
In the End, Everyone is a Kindergartner. 220
Tying It Together: Authentic Communication 220
Key Concepts 222

Chapter 12: The Speaking Experience 223
Preparation is a Process. 224
   Conceptualizing the Speech: One Month in Advance 225
   Visualizing the Speech: Two Weeks Before. 225
   Completing the Speech: One Week Before. 227
   Trusting the Speech: The Night Before. 228
   Delivering the Speech: The Day Of 229
   Recovery 232
   Confidence: Fake It Until You Make It. 234
Tying It Together: Authentic Communication 234
Key Concepts 235

Endnotes. 237

Preface

Public speaking is a platform for authentic communication, the combination of personal perspective, clarity of thought, and audience adaptation. Every person has something unique to contribute to the conversation of the world, their own personal perspective; public speaking empowers us to share that perspective.

But public speaking is not just casual conversation; it involves preparation and planning. This process of preparation forces us to interrogate and clarify our own thinking. Research can challenge our worldview, or strengthen it; organizing our ideas into a clear structure produces moments of insight and inspiration.

Presenting our ideas to others completes this process, and forces us to incorporate others into our own thinking. Adapting to an audience when we research, compose, and deliver our speech exposes us to new perspectives and firmly grounds our ideas in relationships with other individuals and our community.

People often conceptualize public speaking as occurring on a stage in front of two hundred people. Most of us will never deliver such a speech; public speaking shouldn't be artificially limited to this circumstance, or any other. This book aims to break down the walls that people have placed around this activity and open it up to everyone.

In each chapter, you'll find a Speaker's Spotlight. These features share thoughts and advice from people who use public speaking in their everyday lives. From government service to education to public performance, the wide range of experiences that these people have demonstrate how varied public speaking actually is, and hopefully will provide some additional guidance for finding your own voice.

Learning to speak in public is itself a process, one that is daunting to many people. But daunting as it may be, if you work at it, you can master it. This book will help you do just that. It covers the theoretical background of public speaking, but most of its pages are dedicated to practical application: selecting and researching a topic, crafting a speech for maximum effect, refining your physical and vocal delivery, and getting the most out of your performance. Whether you are preparing for your first public performance, or just want a quick refresher before your fiftieth speech this year, this book is for you.

Are you ready to authentically communicate?

CHAPTER 1

Introduction to Public Speaking

Public speaking probably started in prehistory. A hunter killed a huge woolly mammoth, and when he returned home, he assembled his band to regale them with the story of the hunt, filled with details showing that he was a brave, ferocious hunter.

In the 7th or 8th century BCE, a blind poet named Homer memorized his culture's stories about the Trojan War and told them to anyone who would listen. It was the oral tradition that preserved the *Iliad* and the *Odyssey* for future audiences.

Whether an early human boasting about his mammoth conquest, or a blind poet reciting verse about ancient wars, public speaking began with a story, and that's still how it begins today. As children we all told stories. And even with limited vocabulary, we were able to communicate complete, concise ideas through speech. We instinctively called for and sustained the listener's attention. If the listener stopped listening, we spoke louder or repeated important information. And we spoke with a fearlessness and disregard for external disturbances or judgment. A child will tell a story while the phone rings, a dog barks, a car screeches outside, and music plays in the background. The child isn't deterred; she just fights harder to be heard. Fighting to be heard is intuitive. But somewhere between preschool and high school, the fearlessness of childhood often turns into anxiety about speaking in public.

This book is not so much about teaching you how to speak in public as about *reactivating* the knowledge and skills you had as a three-year-old. With these skills, you will again be able to fearlessly present your story. So let's get right to it: it's time to give a speech.

LET'S GIVE A SPEECH

Making a Speech Out of a Story

We're going to begin with story. Stories have a beginning, a middle, and an end. Has anything ever happened to you? Sure it has. Tell us about it. All you need is a beginning, a middle, and an end.

Follow these steps to construct your speech.

1. Choose a simple event that you experienced.

2. In one sentence, summarize the event.

    Example: "I went to the beach."

3. How did the event start?

    Example: "I woke up one morning."

4. What happened during the event?

Example: "I swam in the ocean."

5. How did the event end?

   Example: "The sun went down, and I went home."

6. Add some details to make the story more interesting.

   Example: "It was a really beautiful beach."

Your speech is ready; now it's time to deliver it! Find an audience. Family members will work well; so will a family pet. You just need a focal point. Think about ways to ensure that your beginning, middle, and end will keep your audience interested; use your voice, your facial expressions, and your body. Now go tell them your story.

Congratulations, you just did public speaking! The point is, at its core, public speaking is remarkably simple. It is all around us. In fact, almost everyone has done some form of public speaking. Even if you don't speak in public regularly, you probably know more about public speaking than you think. Let's take a quick inventory of your public speaking experience.

Your Public Speaking Experience

- Have you ever told a story to a group of people?

- Have you ever made a presentation at school or work?

- Have you ever tried to persuade someone about something?

- Have you ever explained how something works?

- Have you ever been impressed by a speaker?

- Have you ever thought someone wasn't very good at public speaking?

- Have you ever watched a political debate?

- Have you ever watched the news?

- Have you ever written an essay?

Chances are, you answered yes to at least a few of those items. All of those everyday experiences help prepare you for public speaking. Speaking, writing, thinking—they all help make us better public speakers. In fact, you probably answered yes to most of those items, but even if you didn't, you can rest assured that you aren't beginning from zero.

What Does It Mean to Speak in Public?

So if we've been publicly speaking since we were very young, and if public speaking is all around us, then why is it a challenge? Well, even though it's been around for so long, people still aren't sure what it is or what they think about it. The phrase "public speaking" conjures up a myriad of images, thoughts, and emotions that are different for each person. Some people get excited about the thought of 25 people paying attention to them; they embrace public speaking as their chance at stardom. Others feel intense fear. Thus, if you asked people what public speaking actually involves, you'd get some wildly varied answers: "applause" and "palms sweating" would both probably be on the list. In fact, surveys have found that public speaking is at the top of people's list of fears; we fear public speaking even more than we fear death.[1] Our fear of public speaking is called communication apprehension, and we will discuss ways of alleviating it in Chapter 3.

Let's try to peel away some of these different perspectives on public speaking and look at the core of what speaking for a listening audience entails. At its most basic, public speaking is speaking to a group of people in a deliberate manner. Here are some general characteristics that make that statement clearer.

- **Public speaking has a beginning, a middle, and an end.** As you just learned, every public speaking event is a process that has a beginning, a middle, and an end. The process begins when the speaker is recognized or introduced and makes her way to the front of the room (or wherever she will speak from). The speaker begins talking, trying to capture the interest of the audience; then the speaker delivers the core of her message and her conclusion. The speech ends when she returns to her seat. (We will cover the components of a speech more in Chapter 4.)

- **Public speaking involves an audience.** Speaking and public speaking are two different things. We often imagine ourselves as noble orators when practicing our speech in front of the mirror. It doesn't take much to convince ourselves that our own ideas are wonderful. Public speaking, however, requires the involvement of an audience. Sometimes our audience is automatically inclined to appreciate our message—a gun rights advocate might have an easy time speaking before the National Rifle Association. On the other hand, there are many occasions when our audience is not primed to appreciate our message. A farmer would have a tough time justifying factory farming to an audience of animal rights activists.

When constructing our message, we need to consider our audience's intellectual predispositions, like their beliefs and biases. It is equally important to consider the finer details about our audience, like whether or not they are anticipating dinner. In Chapter 11, we will talk more specifically about how to adapt your message and your delivery to different audiences.

- **Public speaking combines verbal, vocal, and physical delivery.** When we think about public speaking, we immediately think about words and writing; this is our *verbal* delivery, which will be covered in Chapter 4. But public speaking also involves how we say those words out loud; this is our *vocal* delivery, and will be addressed in Chapter 10. What is sometimes obscured by the phrase "public speaking" is the way we use our bodies to communicate; this is our *physical* delivery, and is addressed in Chapter 9.

When an audience watches a speech, they are taking in the totality of the presentation. The ideas a speaker expresses matter, but the *way* he expresses them and the things he *does* while speaking matter just as much. When most people practice their speech, they have a tendency to focus only on the words. When it is their turn to speak, they feel anxious. Their hands shake because they do not know what they are supposed to do with them, so they clutch the podium, fiddle with their buttons, or jiggle a pen; basically, they invent all sorts of physical coping mechanisms that distract from their message. While rehearsing the vocal performance is critical, considering what the rest of your body is doing while your mouth is moving is also important.

- **Public speaking promotes the ideas of the speaker.** Today, we are free to voice our opinions on Facebook, YouTube, Twitter, Vine, or whatever social media platform becomes popular. In our world, we are given so many platforms to express ourselves that we can easily forget that what we say represents who we are.

For better or worse, audiences assume that a speaker's message represents the speaker's own thoughts and beliefs. In October 2011, country rock icon Hank Williams, Jr., perhaps best known for his performance of "All My Rowdy Friends Are Here on Monday Night" as the opening theme for ESPN's *Monday Night Football*, gave an interview on Fox News in which he said of President Barack Obama's golf outing with House Speaker John Boehner: "It'd be like Hitler playing golf with [Israeli Prime Minister Benjamin] Netanyahu." When Williams was asked to clarify his statement, he responded, "They're the enemy," referring to President Obama and Vice President Joe Biden. Many people were outraged at Williams' comparison of the president to Adolf Hitler. Although Williams later claimed that he was misunderstood, the public had already associated the statement with the country singer. In response to the remarks, ESPN pulled Williams's song from their show. Lesson? Don't compare the president to Hitler. What we say in public represents who we are and what we believe.

Promoting our ideas in public doesn't have to be a bad thing, though. At the 1992 Republican National Convention, Mary Fisher delivered a now famous speech detailing her battle with AIDS and encouraging the party to handle the epidemic with compassion. Even though Fisher was speaking on behalf of millions of men, women, and children across the globe, she was still promoting her own ideas. With the advent of social networking sites and the evolution of newer and easier ways to speak to the public, the lessons we learn from Hank Williams, Jr., and Mary Fisher should inform our interaction with the public.

- **Public speaking represents the culmination of a process called preparation.** We do not necessarily have to prepare ourselves for a casual conversation with our friends. We have built trust with them, and that trust grants us the freedom to say what's on our mind in the moment. Public speaking is different; your audience may not immediately trust you. That trust will have to be earned, and that requires preparation. Even extemporaneous speaking, in which there is little *specific* preparation for the topic, still involves *some* preparation. Students must develop the skill of speaking "off the cuff" by practicing with a variety of topics.

Remember when we said every public speaking event has a beginning, a middle, and an end? Well, you can think about the entire public speaking process as having a beginning, middle, and end. You begin by selecting a topic and compiling research, then you compose, edit, and practice your speech, and you end this process in the moment before the speech. You control your breathing and take a sip of water. You approach the front of a room, confident that you have prepared as best you can, ready to deliver a great speech.

The Purposes of Public Speaking

We can divide the purpose of public speaking into two categories: internal and external purpose. Internal purpose relates to the speaker's experience during the speech: a speaker might want to achieve a performative goal (finish on time, don't stumble) or a goal related to personal advocacy (talk about a difficult topic, express an idea honestly). External purpose relates to the experience of the audience. A speaker might want the audience to experience a particular reaction (joy, sadness, anger) or take a certain action (vote for a candidate, donate to a cause, protest an injustice). Every speech will have some combination of internal and external purposes. Let's take a closer look at some examples of these.

INTERNAL PURPOSES OF PUBLIC SPEAKING

While an audience's reactions are central to the public speaking experience, and while we never want to ignore our audience altogether, there are many reasons to speak in public that have nothing to do with the audience. For instance, many people take public speaking courses simply to conquer their fear of public speaking. Others want to develop skills that will be useful later in life. These goals are internal to the speaker, and there are many examples of them. We speak to:

- **Advocate.** We all care about something. For some of us, it's art or culture; for others, it's politics or policy. Although an audience's reaction may be important, it is sometimes more important that we simply say what we came to say. A filibuster on the Senate floor that has no chance of succeeding might fall into this category.

- **Tell a story.** Remember that funny incident at summer camp you just had to tell everyone about? Like advocacy, some stories are worth telling regardless of your audience's reaction. Eulogies and apologies, for instance, often involve such stories.

- **Learn.** The Roman philosopher Seneca wrote that "by teaching, we learn." The same applies to speaking: when we speak, we process our own ideas and our audience's reaction to those ideas. Speaking can help us put structure to our thoughts; it forces us to present ideas in a clear and coherent way. By speaking about a subject, we learn about it.

- **Grow.** Not only can we learn about a subject when we speak, but we can also learn about ourselves. New experiences teach us something about ourselves; by speaking in public, we can learn to control our bodies, our voices, and our emotions.

SPEAKER SPOTLIGHT

Tony D'Souza
Writer

Tony D'Souza is a novelist and journalist. He is the author of Whiteman, The Konkans, *and* Mule, *receiving praise from The American Academy of Arts and Letters, the* New York Times, Publisher's Weekly, Vanity Fair, *and many others. His work has appeared in* The New Yorker, Esquire, Mother Jones, Salon, Tin House, *and* McSweeney's. *He speaks to audiences regularly about the many different subjects of his work.*

When I talk about my experiences, I know that people are transported to those places and times. It's entertaining for them and me both, because I get to relive things I've done.

No one should ever underestimate the emotional and psychological drain that public speaking is, even when you are comfortable with your material and have already presented it a hundred times.

Speaking to one another is what makes us human, it's how we reveal ourselves to each other.

You have to forget your body and what you look like. You should never say you are nervous but simply plunge into your story. You can't think about people's thoughts about you; you take the space because you deserve it and you tell the story that belongs to you.

Believing you belong up there is the key; having good material is the key to that key.

Often the things I talk about are emotional for me; talking about the Ivorian Civil War is the best example of that—I saw so many horrible things during that period of time. Sometimes, I'll pause and say to the audience, "Do you want to know what it was really like?" That builds intimacy between me and them; they trust that what I will say is private and true. It feels brand new every time.

I recall being nervous many, many years ago, but practice makes perfect and that feeling was long, long ago. I think of it this way: I have something to say. You think I'm a dork or look goofy? I'm going to talk and I'm going to wow you. It's an aggressive feeling for me, even if I don't come across as aggressive. It's a feeling of power and strength.

We all have storytellers to use as examples all through our lives: funny uncles, friends from school. If they tell good stories, figure out how. Good storytellers enjoy their own stories and you can imagine them telling the story to themselves and making themselves laugh even if no one else was around. Good storytellers tell lots of stories. If one fails, they don't worry because they know the next one will work. They fail and they quickly move on.

Stand up and own the stage with your body. Feel the light on you. You may never get it again. Take a few deep breaths and then stand a little taller than you did before. You are up there for a reason. This is an important thing. All of these people want to hear something. Don't waste their time. Start your story with a good strong voice. Own it and make everyone forget about everything else but you.

EXTERNAL PURPOSES OF PUBLIC SPEAKING

We can't always just think about ourselves, though. Public speaking events will almost always have an external purpose, a purpose related to the audience's reaction. When thinking about external purposes, keep your audience's desired reaction at the forefront. Instead of simply saying "I will persuade my audience that I am the best candidate for the job," a politician might say "I will persuade my audience to vote for me on election day." This is a more specific goal that focuses on what the audience will do, think, or feel. There are many types of external purposes; here are some examples:

- **Speaking to persuade.** The goal of persuasive speaking is to get the audience to believe a certain idea that the speaker cares about. The internal purpose of persuasive speeches is to satisfy the speaker's desire to advocate, and the external purpose is to produce a certain reaction from the audience.

    Examples: A lawyer's closing statement, which tries to persuade the jury to acquit her client; a politician, during a debate, trying to persuade the audience to vote for him; or you, trying to get your friends to see the movie you want instead of that stupid new action movie.

- **Speaking to inform.** Informative speaking's goal is to get the audience to understand a certain idea. An external purpose for an informative speech may go beyond getting the audience to understand an idea and actually prepare the audience to perform some task based on that understanding.

    Examples: A teacher delivering a lecture to his students, hoping they do well on the test; an engineer explaining a new product to consumers, hoping they don't accidentally start a fire with it; you trying to explain to your friends why that new action movie is stupid.

- **Speaking to entertain.** The goal of an entertaining speech is to ensure your audience has a good time. These speeches are sometimes called "after dinner speeches," because in olden times people would need some sort of evening entertainment.

  Examples: An emcee at an awards show, hoping the audience isn't bored; a best man delivering a toast at a wedding; you trying to get your friends to like you again after you ruined that new action movie for them.

Tying It Together: Authentic Communication

There are countless other possible purposes for speaking: to memorialize, to confuse, to rebel, to organize, to defame, to become more popular—basically anything you can imagine. These purposes filter and focus the characteristics of public speaking. The beginning, middle, and end of your speech should serve its purposes; your verbal and physical delivery should be tailored to your purposes; your preparation should be geared toward your purposes.

So you've done some good work in this chapter. Remember, public speaking is all around you. By reactivating your own knowledge and experience of public speaking, you can achieve the combination of self-expression and effective communication with an audience that constitutes authentic communication.

Whew, that was a lot. Let's celebrate by doing another speech! This time, think about your own story as a storyteller or speaker. Exploring your own history of speaking will help you understand your strengths and weaknesses. Focusing on times in your life when you have delivered or listened to speeches informs you of the kind of work you need to do as you try to improve as a speaker. It's easier to know where you're going if you know where you've been, so this speech will help frame the rest of the work you do with this book. We're sure that your public speaking history will get more and more interesting as you move through this book.

LET'S GIVE A SPEECH

Constructing A Speech About Your Public Speaking History

Use this timeline to help you construct a speech about your own history as a speaker. Your speech does not have to match the timeline exactly. It is only a guide. Don't forget to add surprising details!

Recall a time you spoke to a group as a child.	Recall a time you spoke to a group at school.	Recall a time you noticed that some-one was a good speaker.	Recall the last time you spoke to a group.	How do you feel about public speaking now?

For fun, we've decided to write our own speaking histories. If you are confused, read our histories to get a better sense of what we are asking you to do.

Public Speaking Book Writer A:
In kindergarten I would pretend that I could speak French; I would just say a lot of nonsense in what, to me, sounded like a French accent. It was a riot, trust me. In middle school, Ms. McNeely, my English teacher, encouraged me to join the debate team when I got to high school. I did. I participated in all sorts of events, and enjoyed them all. In college, I remember seeing a speaker, Robb Telfer, and thinking "this guy is amazing." He was funny, relaxed, and confident. I am a teacher now, and so speaking to groups is part of what I do every day; I still get nervous walking out in front of a new audience, but it's something I've grown accustomed to. I think I am most proud when people tell me that I "speak" just like I talk; that is, I sound like myself. Weird that it took me so long to get to that point.

Public Speaking Book Writer B:
My first memories of speaking in public are as a performer. I was eight years old. I'd organized, recruited, coerced, and blackmailed my cousins into starring in my original adaptation of "Robin Hood and His Merry Men." I, of course, played Robin Hood. After painstakingly rehearsing for all of an hour, I stood before my family, all 27 of them gathered for the holiday, and introduced my work. The next time I remember speaking in public was in school spelling bees. Even though I was only spelling words, I got a nervous feeling from being the center of attention while hundreds of eyes watched me from the cafeteria. The first time I noticed a good speaker, though, was definitely my 5th grade teacher. She told stories in a distinct manner. She made interesting faces and dramatic voices to keep our interest. Then, during middle school, I taught my history class for a day. Preparing the lesson required a lot more work than I thought it would. I had to try to convince the class that I knew what I was talking about. That was hard

to do because my voice and legs would not stop shaking. I am a teacher now, and I speak in public every day. I still get nervous, but I have learned to control my voice and body so they don't shake anymore. I am still trying to convince my classes that I know what I am talking about.

Public Speaking Book Writer C:
The first time I ever spoke in front of a group was when I served as the officiant in a playground wedding in 1st grade. I think the marriage annulled soon afterward. The next time I recall speaking to a group was when I was a child in 6th grade. A kid in my class passed away and I read a poem about him out loud in church. I was the least composed I've ever been in front of that many people in my life, but I got through it and his family said it meant a lot to them. When I first heard Lydia Nelson speak, I felt like I was watching something truly special. She was passionate without being pushy and sincere without being schmaltzy. She was authentic. I speak in front of people all the time now. I get extra nervous the night before, but that motivates me to prepare the best I can for each engagement. Once I'm in front of the room, I remember to breathe, I reassure myself that I'm prepared, and everything falls into place.

Now that you've composed your own story, find an audience and deliver your speaking history. Don't forget to use some of the tools you used earlier to keep your speech interesting: your voice, your facial expressions, and your body.

Key Concepts

- Public speaking is something we all already do; the key is reactivating those skills.

- Public speaking has some basic structures: it involves preparation; it has a beginning, a middle, and an end; and it employs verbal and physical delivery.

- Public speaking has internal purposes, one of which is to promote the ideas of the speaker.

- Public speaking has external purposes, which can be expressed as actions that the speaker wants the audience to take.

CHAPTER 2

Theory of Public Speaking

To better develop a theory of public speaking for our contemporary moment, we need to explore how our understanding of public speaking has evolved throughout history. With each historical era, the purposes, means, style, and theory of public speaking have changed. We've already taken a peek at the history of public speaking: in the last chapter, we took part in the ancient tradition of storytelling. Where did public speaking go from there, though?

In this chapter, we will look at some important eras in the development of public speaking as an art and science and provide a model of understanding communication in a modern context. To be clear, there have been many important moments in the development of public speaking, but we'll be grouping them into four basic eras: Ancient Times, the Classic Era, the Middle Ages and Renaissance, and the Modern Era.[1]

Ancient Times

Nobody knows with any certainty when or where public speaking developed into a *discipline*. We do know, however, that sometime during the late 25th century BCE an Egyptian named Ptah-Hotep wrote down his thoughts on the subject. *The Instructions of Ptah-Hotep* is essentially the world's first self-help book and the first book on public speaking.[2] Near the end of his life, Ptah-Hotep wrote a set of guidelines in an effort to pass down his wisdom to society. He formatted the text so that it would read like a father imparting wisdom to his son. Each rule begins with a hypothetical position in the social hierarchy: "If thou be a priest. . ." or "If thou be a lowly. . ." He believed that you should locate yourself in the world and let that guide how and when you speak your mind.

Ptah-Hotep viewed public speaking as an instrument a speaker could use strategically to gain power. He instructed his son to assess each individual situation to determine what response would produce the most favorable outcome. For example, Ptah-Hotep suggests that you don't say what you really feel about an issue until the powerful person indicates what his opinion is. For Ptah-Hotep, truth was less important than power. While this lesson may seem a little problematic today, the enduring point is that knowing when to speak and what to say when the time comes is a source of power.

We also learn from Ptah-Hotep's instructions that knowing when to listen can be just as powerful as knowing when to speak. Ptah-Hotep argued that listening is both a way of showing respect for the speaker and a strategic practice. Sometimes people say something outrageous or inflammatory, and when they do so, our first instinct is to disagree with them. Instead, Ptah-Hotep suggests that we let others say what they want to say, especially if they are saying something damaging to themselves. Basically, if speech is a sword, it's better to let some-one fall on theirs than for you to strike them down with yours.

The Classical Era

The next two stops on our whirlwind historical tour are ancient Greece and Rome. In the Greek democracy and the Roman republic and empire, public speaking was central to citizen-ship and government.

The Ancient Greeks had a profound influence on public speaking, or rhetoric. They were not only the first Western civilization to produce a refined oral tradition, but they were also the first to extensively theorize about public speaking. The Greeks produced a systematic understanding of rheto-ric and persuasion. The Romans built on what the Greeks had done. Let's look more closely at some of the key thinkers from each society.

THE GREEKS

Our understanding of public speaking owes much to two Greek philosophers: Plato and Aristotle. Plato (428–348 BCE) wrote on many topics—philosophy, religion, logic, ethics, rhet-oric, and even mathematics. Almost all of his writings take the form of public dialogues, so even when he was writing, he was thinking in terms of public speaking. Plato's dialogues treated public speaking as a process for seeking and understanding truth; public speaking was as much about finding consensus as it was about persuading others. Plato was an advocate for *dialectics*, or the process of reasoning and searching for truth through conversation. Like Ptah-Hotep, he emphasized lis-tening as an important part of the public speaking process; unlike Ptah-Hotep, he believed that there was an objective truth that could and should be found through public speaking. He attached less weight to an individual's social status and relationships and more weight to the relationship between the speaker and the truth.

Perhaps more important to the development of public speaking theory was Plato's student, Aristotle (384–322 BCE). While Plato's dialectic approach to philosophy certainly involved public speaking, Aristotle made public speaking the central focus of his study and thought. Aristotle developed a comprehensive approach to rhetoric, which he defined as finding the most persuasive way to develop an argument.

For Aristotle, as for most Greeks of his time, persuasion was the main goal of public speaking;[3] Aristotle wanted to make public speaking a discipline and analyzed it scientifically in order to teach speakers how to persuade. The most important contribution he made was to develop a model of communication, which had five components: the sender, the message, the occasion, the audience, and the effect.

Sender → Message → Occasion → Audience → Effect

1. **Sender**: the speaker.

2. **Message**: the content of the speech.

3. **Occasion**: where, when, why the speech is happening.

4. **Audience**: who is listening to the speech.

5. **Effect**: how the speaker wants the audience to react to the speech.

Let's try to apply it. For the following speeches, do your best to identify each component of Aristotle's model using the brief description of the event.

A. President Abraham Lincoln's Gettysburg Address (http://voicesofdemocracy.umd.edu/lincoln-gettysburg-address-speech-text/).

   Sender:

   Message:

   Occasion:

   Audience:

   Effect:

B. Jon Stewart's commencement address at William and Mary University (http://web.wm.edu/news/archive/index.php?id=3650).

   Sender:

   Message:

   Occasion:

   Audience:

   Effect:

Aristotle believed that the speaker should specifically tailor his speech to each occasion, audience, and desired effect. To find the best means of persuasion, he argued that the speaker must master three key elements: logical reasoning, or logos; a knowledge of character, or ethos; and a knowledge of emotions, or pathos.[4] Let's look more closely at each of these ideas.

- **Logos, or appeal to logic.** Logos relies on internal logic or reasoning to make a point. It was Aristotle's preferred form of persuasion. Let's use logos to persuade someone that she should share her cake with you.

  > You've got an entire cake. You can't possibly eat all of that cake. If you leave part of the cake uneaten, it will go bad. To avoid spoiling the cake, you should give some to me. That way, the cake won't go bad.

  Okay. You set up and finished an argument that makes sense. Your argument relies on moral reasoning and makes some good points.

- **Ethos, or appeal to credibility.** A speaker can use ethos in two ways. The simplest way is to establish the speaker's credentials, or to refer to the credentials of others. For example:

  > I am a professional cake eater; if you want that cake eaten correctly, you should give it to me.

  or

  > Professor Elsworth C. Delicious, of the Culinary Institute's pastry department, has found that cake tastes best when shared. You should share your cake with me.

  Both of these examples attempt to use credibility and authority to get some of the cake. The first establishes the credentials of the speaker, the second relies on the credentials of a third-party expert.

  A more nuanced approach to ethos, though, establishes credibility through tone and purpose. Audiences don't necessarily want to hear a resume from every speaker; more to the point, they are more interested in how the speaker presents herself as a sign of her credibility. For instance, if a speaker makes a series of inappropriate jokes, seems unprepared, or rambles off topic, the audience won't believe that she is a credible source. But if the speaker is focused, serious, and purposeful, she can establish herself as someone worth listening to. Consider:

> I see you have cake; you are a lucky person. Cake is certainly delicious and can bring you a lot of joy. I've had cake once or twice in my day and I definitely enjoyed it every time. I'd be happy to share your cake with you, if you'd like; we could, after all, enjoy it more if we enjoyed together.

This speaker seems to know something about cake; she seems interested in the audience's experience, as if she wanted only to help them enjoy their cake. With sincere and composed delivery, this attempt might convince the audience that this is a person worth sharing a cake with.

- **Pathos, or appeal to emotion.** You can experience a message in many ways: some people think about it, some people argue with it, and some people *feel* it. Pathos, an appeal to emotion, best reaches this third group. When a speaker uses pathos, he appeals not only to the audience's emotion, but also to their imagination and sympathies. For example:

  > When I was five, all I wanted for my birthday was a cake. My family couldn't afford it, though, and I went without. Now I see you have a cake; do you think I might have just a little taste?

  Here, the speaker excites the audience's sympathies. In this instance, the audience may feel sorry for the speaker, but pathos is not always about sadness or sympathy. You can appeal to any emotion. Consider:

> Remember the first time you ever had cake? The joy you felt when you saw it, the delight you felt when you tasted it? Remember the smiles on all your friends' faces as they shared that cake with you, celebrating your birthday? Wouldn't it feel great to capture that happiness again today by sharing your cake with me?

This speaker appeals to the audience's emotions by illustrating how happy they feel about sharing cake, or by appealing to their nostalgia. Pathos can be difficult to deploy, but is often the most powerful means of persuasion.

Using Logos, Ethos, and Pathos

For each of these public speaking occasions, write two or three sentences that would appeal to the audience through logos, ethos, and pathos.

A. You're running for president of student council: convince an auditorium full of students that you deserve the job.

B. You've been accused of cutting the city government's budget: convince us it wasn't you.

C. You've been randomly selected to speak on behalf of the human species to our new alien overlords: convince them to spare us all.

THE ROMANS

We now move forward in time (and west along the Mediterranean) to the Roman republic and an orator and rhetorician named Cicero (106–43 BCE). He was considered the finest orator of his generation and also Rome's most significant scholar of rhetoric and oratory. He championed the Greek approach to rhetoric, favoring a dignified, simple style of speaking. He believed that oratory was immensely important in civic life because as a lawyer and politician he had participated in numerous trials and public hearings and seen the power of public speaking firsthand. Cicero argued that orators must be well-rounded thinkers in order to fully engage in any subject; he also believed that "good men" must train to be great orators, so that they could oppose "evil men" in political endeavors. He developed an understanding of persuasive speaking that became known as the five canons: invention, arrangement, style, memory, and delivery.

About a hundred years after Cicero's death, Quintilian (35-100 CE) wrote about oratory and rhetoric. Where Cicero was a great orator, Quintilian was a great teacher. His 12-volume book, *Institutio Oratoria,*[5] which broke down the ideal, complete education of a model orator, is still considered one of the best guides to public speaking. Quintilian rejected the flowery, ornate rhetoric that was popular in his time, and instead embraced the simple, direct language of Cicero and the Greeks. Quintilian's most important contribution was refining the five canons of rhetoric first developed by Cicero.

The Five Canons of Rhetoric
as demonstrated by Jim's speech to the chess club

Invention: Coming up with ideas for a speech.

Jim: "We need to buy new chessboards, so our club can practice."

Arrangement: Ordering and structuring the ideas.

Jim: "1. Chess is fun. 2. Boards would let us play chess. 3. We can have fun!"

Style: Determining how to persuasively present the ideas.

Jim: "I'll use exciting stories of chess matches to get my audience excited!"

Memory: Memorizing the speech.

Jim: "I'll memorize every morning and evening. . ."

Delivery: Delivering the speech.

Jim: "And that excitement, friends, is why we should invest in some new chessboards!"

Middle Ages and Renaissance

During the decline of the Roman Empire, a bright rhetorical scholar ushered in a new era of public speaking. His name was St. Augustine of Hippo (354–430 CE), one of Western history's most influential philosophers. When he was young, Augustine was introduced to one of the few works of Cicero that was available at that time, *Hortensius* (which is now lost), and developed an interest in the study and teaching of rhetoric. Following his conversion to Christianity, Augustine began writing seriously about public speaking, which he saw as a powerful weapon in spreading the Christian faith and defending orthodox doctrine against heresy. In his works on rhetoric, Augustine changed the direction of oratory from civic to religious purposes, from politics to preaching.[6]

Unlike Cicero, who thought public speaking was a skill reserved for the elite, Augustine viewed rhetoric as a skill that almost anyone can learn. He reasoned that just as babies learn to speak by hearing others, young people can learn public speaking by emulating the practices of more eloquent public speakers. Because anyone could learn how to craft and deliver a persuasive message—even those who might use rhetoric to spread false doctrine—Augustine believed that it was the duty of Christian leaders and teachers to become great speakers so that they could defend what he saw as the truth.

For almost a thousand years after Augustine, political and religious unrest combined with disease and famine, causing major crises across Europe during which many classical writings were lost and scholarship centered around the church and religious orders. The era concluded in the 14th century with a new period of scientific, artistic, and academic growth known as the Renaissance. During this period, scholars known as Humanists wanted all people, including women, to be equipped with skills to speak their minds and engage in their community. These individuals, some of whom were high-ranking church officials, encouraged the spread of information so that everyone (not just members of religious orders) could seek the truth and persuade others to do the same.

At the end of the 15th century, the moveable type printing press was developed in Europe, and people became obsessed with the written word. They became more interested in understanding rhetoric from a written context than from a performative one, so scholars became less and less interested in teaching memory and style and more and more interested in the crafting of language.

Modern Era

The modern era of public speaking, which began as the Renaissance came to a close in the 17th century, has been defined more by changes in society and technology than by any individual thinkers. The pace of change has accelerated (and there are many small changes happening all the time). We'll focus on the three most important for public speaking: developments in science, the evolution of the economy, and the telecommunications revolution.

SCIENCE

The Scientific Revolution of the 17th and 18th centuries radically changed the way we view public speaking. Scientists and thinkers stressed the importance of observation and experimentation over tradition and faith in explaining the world. In the wake of that revolution, a new scientific discipline emerged that had a significant impact on our understanding of public speaking. In the late 1800s, the Germans and Austrians developed a scientific approach to psychology. This new discipline enabled a greater variety and depth of audience analysis. If psychologists could understand and explain the psychological motivations of people, then speakers could use that knowledge to craft speeches that were appropriate for each distinct audience.

More fundamentally, the very idea of psychology meant that speakers had to reevaluate their approach to persuasion in general. The audience was no longer an undifferentiated mass waiting to accept or reject a speaker's message based solely on how "persuasive" it was. Instead, the audience might accept or reject the speaker's message for their own, personal reasons. The psychological perspective suggests that, when preparing, the speaker must consider the needs and desires of the audience.

The scientific study of communication also contributed to the development of public speaking. Researchers could now quantify and study various questions about public speaking: Does persuasion work? How do audiences react to different types of messages? These questions could now be answered through observation and data analysis, leading to new advances in communication theory and new ways of understanding what makes public speaking effective.

ECONOMICS

New knowledge produced through the scientific revolution, combined with a rise in literacy, required new public speaking skills for many traditional jobs. Craftsmen, architects, bankers, explorers, and artists all had to learn to communicate with the public more efficiently and effectively.

Advancements in technology and education also led to jobs that Ptah-Hotep could never have imagined. New technology required specialists to explain the technology to the public. New methods of mass communication led to the rise of the advertising and public relations industries. A more educated and literate public created the market for newspapers and other forms of press. Public speaking became a point of emphasis in education, not just for classicists or humanities students, but also for business and accounting majors. The ability to speak in public was no longer distinguished as a necessary skill for clergy, royalty, or the governing elite, but for every citizen. This, in turn, led to an increase in the practical study of and interest in public speaking.

MEDIA

The third important development of the modern era has been the invention and explosion of telecommunications. Every advance in communication technology has had significant effects on the way we personally communicate. Recording devices, telephones, radio, television, text messaging, and video chat have all had an enormous impact on public speaking. Recording devices allowed people to hear their own voices for the first time; telephones and radio delivered a speaker's voice directly to our homes. Consequently, the way we used our voices to communicate was suddenly under a more intense scrutiny. Radio and television brought communication to mass audiences. Speakers were able to reach larger audiences than they ever had before, meaning they had to tailor their delivery to appeal to larger groups. Even something as seemingly simple as a microphone and amplifier meant that speakers no longer had to strain to be heard; speakers could now speak casually, more informally, and have their voice projected to everyone in the audience.

Changes in media have also made public speaking less formal. We are so accustomed to personally tailored content that we expect speakers to speak only to us. Audiences are more mobile and powerful than ever; if people don't like something someone says, they can just change the channel or "unfriend" them. Or, they can make fun of them in their mobile status, or tweet, or away message. This evolution of audience power created a deeper responsibility for speakers to adapt to their audiences, so it's a good thing they have a variety of new tools available to help them out.

Nadir Joshua
Attorney

Nadir Joshua is a lawyer, and he lived in Brooklyn, twice. He worked at two large law firms, and also spent some time as an attorney in New York City government. He recently moved to the West Coast to join the employment law team of a tech company. Nadir embodies our belief that public speaking is a process—something that gets easier every time we do it.

The opportunity to share ideas with an audience is the core of public speaking.

I think most public speaking is done on a small scale—in conversations and meetings. There are times when I am required to give presentations, but mostly my day-to-day public speaking is in small groups.

Learning how to organize ideas, to make them easily understood, is about as important a skill as anyone can have. It will structure your thoughts, change the way you listen, and make you a better writer.

When Bill Clinton eulogized Ossie Davis (http://www.democracynow .org/2005/2/14/remembering_ossie_davis_1917_2005_maya), he said what I thought at the time were the kindest things that could be said about someone's death.

Effective public speaking should leave you with a feeling. It should make you want to do something better or be something better.

The best way to get good at public speaking is to speak in public. Do it every chance you get.

Where Does That Leave Us

Modern communication theory has built on earlier thinkers and developments to devise a holistic model of communication. We've learned that communication can be broken down into seven components: the source, the speaker, the message, the medium, the audience, feedback, and interference.

The *source* is the origin of the idea, information, or concept that the speaker will communicate. The *speaker* interprets the source by applying his unique perspective, understanding, and experiences, converting the source into a *message*. Even if they are working from the same source, different speakers may produce different messages. For example: two speakers are tasked with describing a movie, but they may only use plot information from the film and may not verbalize their own values or criticisms. Each speaker will use his own perspective, understanding, and experiences to shape how the film is portrayed; he will choose different plot information to represent the film, and the choices will reflect how the speaker thought about it.

The speaker will have to use a *medium*, or a method to communicate. If a speaker is communicating over the radio, then the medium is radio broadcast. If the speaker is communicating by way of microphone at a press conference, then the medium is the microphone.

On receiving the speaker's message, the *audience* decodes the message using their own perspective, understanding, and experiences. The audience then encodes its own message and sends *feedback* to the speaker. Audience feedback is an important indicator of how effectively the speaker is communicating, and this feedback can take many forms: an audience member can nod his head if he agrees with the speaker, or he can close his eyes and take a little nap if he is bored. Sometimes a listener will clap if he hears something exciting, and sometimes he will laugh if he thinks the message is funny.

If clapping or laughing becomes excessive, they can become *interference*, which is a circumstance that disrupts the reception of the speaker's message. There are three types of interference: internal, external, and speaker-generated. *Internal interference* is generated by the listener herself: she may be distracted, or tired, or anxious to leave and get on with her day. *External interference* comes from the environment, or the setting of the speech. Maybe there is a thunderstorm or the air conditioner is buzzing, or the room smells like old shoes. These factors can make it difficult for both the audience and the speaker to focus. A lack of focus can be a source of *speaker-generated interference*. A speaker may lose his train of thought, gesture wildly, or stumble over his words; all of these can distract from his message and interfere with communication.

Of course, the lines between the different types of interference and also between interference and feedback can be blurry. If a hornet is flying around the auditorium, there's going to be all types of interference. The external interference (the hornet) will produce internal interference (the audience focuses on the hornet) and speaker-generated interference (the speaker is terrified of hornets and stumbles over his words).

Feedback from one audience member may constitute interference for another. When Iraqi journalist Muntazer al-Zaidi threw a shoe at President George W. Bush, or when Representative Joe Wilson shouted "You lie!" during President Barack Obama's State of the Union address, they were providing feedback; for the rest of the audiences at these events, and for the speakers themselves, these actions constituted interference.

Each public speaking event will have a unique source, speaker, message, medium, audience, feedback, and interference. If a speaker knows the factors that shape the public speaking experience, then the speaker can better prepare her message(s), taking control of whether or not her message will be received in the desired manner.

Tying It Together: Authentic Communication

Even though the world is ever-changing, the core elements of public speaking have remained consistent. The same elements that were addressed by ancient philosophers are what modern speakers are working with. These classic thinkers remain relevant because their advice is still true today. That's why, when you read their words, you tilt your head and think, "Huh, that *is* true." The instructions of Ptah-Hotep, Plato, Aristotle, Cicero, Quintilian, and St. Augustine are still applicable. Listening, considering your audience, finding the best means of persuasion, and preparing for different occasions are still important. There is still a message, a medium, feedback, and interference. And the face of both the sender and the recipient of the message has not changed all that much. Yesterday's speakers didn't look all that different than the speakers today.

Ultimately, the speaker will always be a person with something to say, and the audience will always be a group of people more or less willing to listen. Authentic communication is striking a compromise between speaker and audience. Audience adaptation is important, and we will discuss it in Chapter 11. For now, though, it's more important to remember that as speakers we are in control of our own destinies; we can achieve the outcomes we want by taking control of the source of our ideas, making those ideas our own, and sending them to the audience in our own way. Whether we are seeking truth, power, or knowledge, the tools and strategies discovered in the past will help us shape our future.

Making an Introduction Speech

This chapter covers a lot of ground, but let's make sure we apply some of it to our public speaking practice. In this exercise, you will explore the modern communication model by generating a short speech of introduction.

Step 1: Use the questions below to generate your *source*. After you answer the questions, compose three to five sentences that will be your *message*.

- What is your name? _____

- Where do you live? _____

- What is a favorite hobby that you have?

  _____

- What is a favorite book, song, movie, or video game?

  _____

Step 2: Now, choose a *medium* and a target *audience* from below. The audience can be real or imaginary: you decide. Choose one of each.

Medium	Audience
Face to face	Parent(s)
Over the phone	Friend(s)
Through video chat	A television studio audience
Voice recording	A journalist
Video recording	A cyborg from the future

Step 3: Deliver your Introduction Speech as you have prepared it.

Key Concepts

- Ptah-Hotep, the first known author of theory about public speaking, believed public speaking to be a tool for acquiring power.

- Plato believed in a dialectic, truth-seeking approach to public speaking.

- Aristotle developed the first model of public speaking and divided the means of persuasion into three categories: logic (logos), credibility (ethos), and emotion (pathos).

- Quintilian admired the plain, powerful style of Cicero and refined Cicero's five canons of rhetoric: invention, arrangement, style, memory, and delivery.

- Augustine believed anyone could speak well if they were well prepared.

- The Modern Era brought about many changes in public speaking through the development of science, the change in the economy, and the rise of telecommunications.

- The contemporary model of public speaking has seven components: source, speaker, message, medium, audience, feedback, and interference.

CHAPTER 3

Overcoming Communication Apprehension

We are always wary about referring to public speaking as a *skill*, but surely that's what it is: the developed and practiced ability to do something well. And like any skill—carpentry, sewing, playing the piano—public speaking can be improved with practice.

Public speaking is also a process, one that involves many skills. Just like carpentry is about more than swinging a hammer or using a saw, public speaking is about more than just speaking loudly or doing research. The individual skills will certainly help—but only if you understand how they all fit together. The catch is, learning each skill and how they are linked can be a difficult process. That means you're likely to experience some degree of failure while learning. Since failure is a part (the most important part) of learning, it shouldn't scare us. But it does.

The fear of public speaking is strange, because public speaking is sort of just talking, and talking is something we've done since we were very young. So when we are in front of an audience and our bodies and voices and nerves suddenly betray us, we can feel a very personal sense of failure. This, in turn, can cause us to fear speaking in public. As we learned, this fear is known as communication apprehension, and it is very common.

This chapter will describe some common forms of communication apprehension and provide some strategies for dealing with them. All of the advice, though, comes back to the basic idea of public speaking as a process. When a speaker understands this and approaches public speaking as such, she can undertake learning how to speak in public with a little more optimism.

Embrace the Nervous, Dispatch the Worry

Mark Twain famously said: "There are two kinds of speakers: those that are nervous and those that are liars." Everyone gets nervous. Everyone is worried they will be embarrassed. And you know what? Sometimes you might get embarrassed. But being embarrassed might not always be such a bad thing.

When you get embarrassed, embrace it. Dacher Keltner, a professor of psychology at the University of California, Berkeley, has found that when a speaker experiences embarrassment, when the speaker feels it is the worst moment of his life, the audience actually likes the speaker more.[1] An instance of embarrassment exposes us as human, and so the audience trusts us and is more likely to accept our message. That so many people fear public speaking means the audience *knows* what you are doing is hard. They are on your side. So when you trip up, embrace it. Have a laugh with the audience and move along in your presentation as one of them. Often, an embarrassing moment can release tension and unify the speaker and audience, so the speech becomes more like a conversation.

Getting nervous is part of being human; the authors speak in public all the time as teachers and performers, and we still get nervous. We worry about our performance just like other speakers, and we have assembled a list of the worries that we have suffered through or otherwise encountered in our collective public speaking experience. But we don't want *you* to worry, so we've described some common worries and offered some advice on how to overcome them.

I'M WORRIED THAT I'LL PASS OUT

Do you get a sick feeling in the pit of your stomach when you even think about speaking in front of an audience? Do your hands shake when you stand in front of the classroom? Does your voice tremble when you realize people are actually listening to you?

Well, there is a very good reason why you might be feeling this way. Our bodies have a complicated network of nerves called the autonomic nervous system (ANS) that regulates our internal organs and glands. One component of the ANS is the sympathetic nervous system, which is responsible for all of the instinctive, unconscious reactions our bodies make to dangers or threats. When your body registers that it is in danger, it activates this "fight or flight" system. The queasy feeling in your stomach and your shaky hands when you get up to speak is your nervous system sending biofeedback to your brain telling you SOMETHING REALLY BAD IS GOING TO HAPPEN!

How to Deal

- **Prepare for the event, not just the speech.** The morning of the big speech, eat a light breakfast. You burn a lot of calories when you speak, so even if you aren't a breakfast person, you should try to eat something. Notice we used the word "light." You don't want to eat a huge breakfast the morning of your big presentation. Instead, eat an apple or a granola bar.

  Give yourself plenty of time prior to the engagement. Don't compound your speaking anxiety with anxiety about being late. Wake up with enough time to have breakfast and rehearse your speech. This will help jumpstart your memory and make you feel more confident in your performance.

  Finally, and there's no delicate way to say this, use the restroom. We don't mean to make things awkward, but there are a few good reasons to use the restroom before you speak. Remember that sympathetic nervous system we talked about? The one responsible for your fight or flight reactions? One fight or flight reaction is, well, you get the idea. In addition to helping relieve some physiological tension, giving yourself a brief bathroom pep talk never hurts.

- **Trust yourself and focus on breathing.** Some of the worst anxiety strikes when you are in the audience, waiting to present, and maybe even watching others present before you. When you feel anxious, your breathing becomes shallower and your heart rate spikes. Concentrate on taking deep, even breaths. Deep breathing will return your heart rate to normal and that will calm your nerves. Who knows, you might actually enjoy your fellow speakers more.

Also, trust yourself and your preparation process. Don't pull out your speech while others are presenting. In addition to being rude, trying to get one last moment of practice in before your speech will only increase your anxiety. Trust that you have worked hard to prepare your speech and be confident in your performance.

- **Control your performance with poise and pace.** Your performance begins before you start speaking; it begins as you take the stage. When you first approach the front of the room, smile and look at your audience before you say your first words. This will ensure that everyone in the audience is ready for you to begin. When the audience is ready to listen to you speak, they are less inclined to engage in distracting behaviors like digging in their bag to get another peek at their speech.

  Also, slow down. Anxious speakers have a tendency to speed through their speeches in order to get them over with. However, doing so often increases the instances of flubs and fluency breaks that *worsen* anxiety. Think of your performance as a car on a country drive. There are going to be hills and valleys. Simply tearing through your speech is like removing the brakes from the car. You lose control and crash. So, slow down your rate and don't forget to breathe.

I'M WORRIED I'LL FORGET WHAT TO SAY

Our brains have a funny habit of forgetting important things: where we left our keys, our best friend's birthday, the password to our bank account. They are also notorious for forgetting our speech the moment we walk to the front of the room. There's a good explanation for this: our memory is context-dependent. When something happens to us that our brain deems memorable, it encodes other contextual information as well. Studying deep sea divers, psychologists D. R. Godden and Alan Baddeley found that the environment has a lot to do with our ability to recall information. Their divers were more likely to forget things they saw under the water once they returned to the surface.[2] When people tell you to "retrace your steps" to find your lost DVD, they are encouraging you to activate your context-dependent memory. Walking yourself through the context present during the encoding of the memory (putting down your DVD) can aid in the recovery of the memory.

When you memorize your speech, your brain is absorbing the context in which you are memorizing. If you practice in the shower, then you will become a pro at delivering your speech in the shower. But when you then stand before a sea of people, it's easy to forget your speech because your brain is not used to that context.

How to Deal

- **Make context-dependent memory work for you.** Since people memorize based on context, you should ideally memorize and practice your speech in contexts that are similar to the actual performance. When preparing for speeches or debates, politicians almost always visit the space where they will be speaking beforehand. If you will be speaking in an auditorium, try to practice in an auditorium; if you will be speaking before an audience, memorize and practice in front of an audience.

  If you can't recreate or approximate the context in which you will be performing, then vary the contexts in which you memorize. This will enable your brain to focus on the content of the speech rather than the narrow context in which you practice. So don't just memorize in the shower;

memorize in the hallway, in the front yard, at the museum, and on the train as well.

And don't just vary the location; vary the *way* you memorize. Practice walking and standing still; practice with gestures and without; practice with notes and without. This variation will equip you for any situation.

- **Don't just memorize your material; master it.** Many speakers approach a speech as just a set of words recorded on paper; they neglect the ideas behind those words. A better tactic is to master the ideas of a speech, which makes the specific wording less important. There's science to support this approach! Cognitive psychologists Fergus Craik and Robert Lockhart developed a model of memory known as "levels of processing." They argue that when we deeply process material and make connections between it and other ideas, we are better able to remember that material.[3] If you know what idea you are trying to communicate, and if you truly understand that idea, you will be able to remember it and communicate it effectively.

So don't just focus on the words; spend time examining and thinking about the ideas of the speech. Revisit your research and try to learn more about your subject material.

Working On Memory
Memory is a skill that can be improved with practice. Here are a few quick exercises to help.

- Select two sentences from a book or magazine and give yourself one minute to memorize them; try the exercise again with another two sentences and see if you can do it in less time.

- Select five sentences to memorize and, as you read them, assign them each a symbol (sentence 1 = rhinoceros, sentence 2 = Egypt, etc.). See if you can remember the sentences by remembering the order of symbols.

- Try memorizing a list or a well-known set of objects, like all the elements of the periodic table or all the countries in Europe. See which items are easier or harder to memorize and think about what connections your brain makes as you memorize or recite the list.

I'M WORRIED PEOPLE WON'T UNDERSTAND WHAT I HAVE TO SAY

Sometimes, speakers are tasked with explaining a difficult concept: quantum physics or Aristotelian logic. These topics can be complex, and trying to explain them can cause a lot of anxiety. Will the audience "get it"? Will they ask questions? Will they *not* ask questions and just walk away confused?

You make this anxiety worse if you think you don't understand your own speech. But remember, as discussed in Chapter 1, every speaking event is a great opportunity for the speaker to learn more about the topic. When we speak, we learn. Sometimes, though, speakers can be overwhelmed by their topic and that apprehension actually stifles learning.

How to Deal

- **Use your thesis to narrow and control your preparation.** Lazy thesis writing can lead to confused preparation and rambling speeches; without adequate focus, you can quickly get lost in too much information. For example, organizing a speech about sharks in general would be very difficult, but if you narrow your topic to "The most common species of sharks" or "How sharks hunt their prey," your preparation becomes more manageable.

Writing a well-defined thesis will help guide your research and give you a sense of what you need to cover. It helps to eliminate the pressure to learn everything about the topic. With a better handle on preparation, you are more likely to feel confident about your speech.

- **Prepare beyond your topic.** Mark Twain also said, "It usually takes me more than three weeks to prepare a good impromptu speech." It takes an immense amount of preparation to speak on even a narrow subject for just a short time. But that preparation is worth it. After you develop a sense of what you will cover, expanding your preparation a bit beyond the narrowed scope of your speech can provide context for you and your audience and can help you anticipate questions and points of confusion. As discussed earlier, mastering your material also helps with the memorization process.

- **Emphasize clear structure.** Sometimes, a speaker will over-explain ideas, making them more complicated than is necessary. Although he has already thought about how best to present his ideas, when he gives his speech he panics and adds extra information. Because these ideas are spur-of-the-moment, they aren't clear, and so he panics more.

During preparation, a speaker must work to eliminate unnecessary sentences and communicate clearly and concisely. By using clear previews, reviews, transition statements, and structural language, she can help the audience follow her ideas. Even if the content of the speech is difficult or unfamiliar to the audience, a speaker can emphasize the connective material of the speech to keep it accessible. Consider this example:

> Now let's turn our attention to the next important feature of the African elephant: its proboscis, its trunk. The trunk serves three basic functions: breathing, grasping, and sound production.

This example contains several useful structural elements. It has a transition statement (Now let's turn our attention to. . .); it defines difficult terms (proboscis, or trunk); and it previews future information (three basic functions). This structural language, which surrounds the content, not only gives the audience time to process and organize new information, but also helps the audience anticipate what will come next. There are many ways to add or refine structure; we will cover this more thoroughly in Chapter 4.

I'M WORRIED PEOPLE WON'T LIKE WHAT I HAVE TO SAY

Humans are social by nature, and we want the audience to love us. We want approval, we want applause, we want a standing ovation. Sometimes, though, we're not sure if we're going to get it. Maybe we'll be speaking in front of a hostile audience or taking an unpopular stance; or maybe we just aren't confident in what we have to say. If we are uncertain of whether an audience will approve of what we are saying, we assume they are judging us, and that can cause a lot of anxiety.

How to Deal

- **Know that your audience is more likely to be disinterested than anything else.** A disinterested audience is willing to suspend judgment; they are willing to listen to the speaker on her own terms. Very few audiences have already arrived at decisions about the issues speakers address; fewer audiences are unwilling to entertain the ideas that the speaker presents. In our experience, most audiences understand that effective listening means limiting their personal biases about a subject.

- **Know that your audience isn't an undifferentiated mass.** Even if *some* people in the audience disagree with you, others are likely to support what you say. You might imagine some faceless mob bearing torches and throwing stones, but that's not how audiences work. Audiences are made up of individuals, and each audience member will have a unique response to your speech. This is an important thought to remember. Imagine a speaker discussing the prevalence of sexual violence on a college campus. This speech might meet with resistance from the general college audience, who may feel that the speech makes the college look bad, but for any victims of sexual violence in that audience, that speaker may be making a huge difference. If some people in the audience don't like what you have to say, so be it; maybe you're not speaking for those people.

- **Say what you want to say and *want* to say what you say.** We are much more willing to endure negative feedback if we are invested in our topic: a subject that is personally important or that we feel could be important for others. The potential disapproval of an audience can be disheartening enough; don't aggravate it by presenting a position you don't support. The courage of your convictions can go a long way in relieving anxiety. If you believe in what you say, you have a stronger reason for speaking.

I'M WORRIED ANOTHER SPEAKER WILL BE BETTER THAN ME

Some ways in which we are compared to other people bother us more than others. If we were asked to run a one hundred meter race against Usain Bolt, considered the world's fastest person, we'd be okay with losing. He's faster than we are, so what? It doesn't reflect on our personal sense of self-worth. But other potential areas for comparisons, like a public speaking event, seem to disturb us more easily. Admittedly, there is something intensely personal about speaking in public, and this anxiety is worsened when a speech will be judged alongside another.

How to Deal

- **Know that public speaking is an acquired skill, not an inherent talent.** Babies do not enter this world as polished, powerful orators. Speaking well takes practice. Other speakers may be better than you; it is a near certainty that you will encounter other people who have developed this skill to a higher level. That's the thing: it is a skill, developed by a process of preparation, and anyone can improve.

- **Admire other speakers and learn from their performances.** Remember that skills reflect experience; if another speaker has more experience, so be it. Appreciate the work she has put into her craft and use her performance as an example to aspire to. There are no final evaluations in life. Every public speaking event is a chance to learn something that will be useful in the next public speaking event, and if not in the next public speaking event, then in some other context. If you can turn a public speaking event into an opportunity to grow and embrace the role of a lifelong learner, then your anxiety will decrease.

- **Reflect on each performance, and make your first comparison with yourself.** Just as we can learn from other speakers, we can learn from ourselves. Each performance is another piece of data to study; every experience is worthwhile, but reflection makes experience exponentially more valuable. It's not only healthier to focus on your own performance, but much more practical; sometimes another speaker's style or approach may be so different from your own that you can learn very little from him.

SPEAKER SPOTLIGHT

Saya Hillman
Founder of Mac & Cheese Productions

Through weekend getaways, two-hour workshops, three-month classes, and speaking engagements, Saya helps her clients have a blissfully rewarding life. She was one of Brazen Careerist's Top Twenty Young Professionals to Watch, has been featured in Forbes *and the* New York Times, *and is a TEDx speaker. Saya advises to talk about what you know to help with communication apprehension.*

A few years ago, I decided being a "Professional Speaker" looked like a great way to make a living and gain exposure for my company. I threw a "Hire me to speak" page up on my website, and two days later I had my first paid speaking gig—a design conference for 300 attendees at the Museum of Contemporary Art.

I teach workshops in areas that others are interested in: how to find fulfillment in life and how to be productive, organized, and efficient.

The chance that you will speak in front of others at least once in your life, if not three, fifty, or hundreds of times, is pretty high. So why not get to the point where it isn't a source of fear or a reason you beat yourself up?

The desire to connect human to human is strong, and if you have the ability to make people feel good about themselves and help them create community with one another—which public speaking often does—you'll be a rock star.

My TEDx talk was nerve-wracking both because it was, ya know, TED! And also because we weren't allowed to use notes. While I had spoken numerous times before, I had never done so without the security blanket of notes. Twelve minutes up there naked?!? Eek! While there were a few stumbles and bumbles, I did it, and relatively successfully I think. And now I know I can do it whenever I need to.

If you talk about what you know and what you're passionate about, there's MUCH less stress than if you talk about something that's not in your field of expertise.

While some people feel more comfortable speaking in front of people they know, I'd much rather do it in front of strangers. So my ideal gigs, especially at the start, were in front of audiences I knew didn't know me.

Take improv! So helpful in becoming a more confident and captivating speaker.

Tying It Together: Authentic Communication

When you speak in front of an audience, you become keenly aware of what's involved in speaking. Your mouth may feel dry. Your tongue may twist in knots. Your lips may quiver. You can be easily overwhelmed. If you experience speech anxiety, remember that it is just your body telling you that you have something important to say. It's natural to feel this sort of anxiety. When this happens, return to and strengthen your process of preparation and reflection. Harness this anxiety, incorporate it into your process, and watch the moment you understand public speaking turn into the moment you deliver your message with confidence.

LET'S GIVE A SPEECH

Speaking in Different Contextual Environments

To help alleviate communication anxiety, you will practice adapting to new circumstances when you speak. Follow the instructions to take the next step in your communication process.

Step 1: Construct a speech.

A. Write down *one worry* mentioned in this chapter that most closely resembles something that you have experienced.

B. Use the worry to complete this speech template. Be brave and rewrite it in your own words.

   1. Hello. My name is (*insert name*) and I have a worry about public speaking. My worry about public

speaking is (*insert worry*). Recently, I read about how to address my worry.

2. In the book the authors say to (*enter 1 piece of advice given to address your chosen worry*). They also say to (*enter another piece of advice given to address your chosen worry*).

3. So, in conclusion, I will incorporate (*insert advice*) in my speechwriting process so I will no longer suffer from (*insert worry*).

Step 2: Memorize your speech using the suggestions for memorizing above.

Step 3: Create an audience.
Remember, you are practicing, so you will use a practice audience. Choose a favorite inanimate object to be your audience. You can choose a favorite stuffed animal, picture—anything.

Step 4: Deliver your speech to your audience.

Step 5: Change the context of your performance.
Add another audience member (another inanimate object), and deliver your speech in a different position or room.

Step 6: Change the context of your performance ... again!
Add a third audience member (another inanimate object), and deliver your speech in yet another position, angle, or room. This time, be creative. Try speaking in the shower, where your voice will echo, or outdoors, where your voice will not carry well.

Hopefully, you noticed that each speaking experience was different. When you practice speeches, try to rehearse in different places so that you are prepared for any surprise or anxiety attack.

Key Concepts

- Public speaking is a process composed of many skills.

- Public speaking skills are acquired through experience.

- Feeling a moderate amount of anxiety about public speaking is natural and even desirable.

- Memory is context-dependent, so memorize and practice your speeches in multiple settings.

- Focus on your process of preparation and reflection in order to improve as a public speaker.

CHAPTER 4

Writing for the Listening Audience

Every time you speak, you have an audience in front of you. Those audiences may vary wildly: maybe you are speaking to the Midwestern Banker's Association, to the 34th Street Park Improvement Committee, or to a class of high school students. Chapter 11 will explain how to analyze and adapt your presentation to specific audiences; right now, though, we will focus on what all of these audiences have in common: they are all "listening" audiences. They cannot read your speech; they can only listen to it. This means that the way you compose your speech will be different from the way you would write it for a "reading" audience. This chapter will explore how to adapt your writing for a listening audience as you prepare for a public speaking event. But first, we need to establish something about audiences.

Audiences Are Easily Distracted

Holding the audience's attention takes effort and focus. Although many factors can increase an audience's motivation (and we will cover many of these in the later chapters), many remain beyond the speaker's control. Audiences may be tired; they may have somewhere to be; they may be thinking about what they will make for dinner or they may hear a siren in the distance. There is a literal universe of possible obstacles for which the speaker cannot foresee or prepare.

The good news, though, is that understanding some basic strategies will help you more easily hold your audience's attention.

Defining the Listening Audience

A listening audience differs from a reading audience in that a listening audience has much less control over how it receives the message. You learned in Chapter 2 that a message is always competing with three types of interference: external, internal, and speaker-generated. A reading audience can reduce external interference, like car horns, by choosing a different time or place to read. A reading audience can also exert some control over internal interference, like daydreams or worries, by setting the reading aside until they are more focused. A reading audience can even overcome "speaker-generated" interference, like poor or confusing writing, through persistence or re-reading.

A listening audience, by contrast, is relatively powerless to reduce interference. Externally, listening audiences cannot get up in the middle of a speech and adjust the settings on a screechy microphone. Similarly, if the venue has poor acoustics or if there are distracting noises, such as crying infants or barking dogs, the audience cannot simply leave.

Internal interference is also difficult to avoid because the speaker will not (or cannot) wait until the audience is more focused. And whatever interference is generated by the speaker herself—a verbal stumble, distracting physical gestures, or confusing structure—leaves the audience in a difficult spot; audience members can't stand up and yell "Hey! Slow down! And stop doing that thing with your hands, it's distracting!"

Structuring a Speech for the Listening Audience

By understanding and anticipating interference, speakers can overcome it. The first way to do so is to effectively organize your speech; effective organization is critical to ensuring you get your message across. An effectively organized speech includes the following:

- **A purpose.** You need a reason for speaking. Your audience's first thought when you stand up to speak will likely be "Who is this person and what is he doing?" Since they're asking this question, it's best that you have an answer. Let's say you wanted to inform the audience about how to properly brush a pony. To ensure that your audience understands this message you would compose a purpose statement, "To inform the audience about how to brush a pony." You won't necessarily include the purpose statement in your speech, but writing down the purpose statement helps you conceptualize the style of speech (informative) and to narrow the topic of the speech (brushing ponies).

- **An introduction.** Actually, make that a *killer* introduction. The introduction captures the attention of the audience with an Attention-getting Device (AGD) and provides context for the topic of your speech. Your introduction may include an interesting story or shocking statistic. The introduction will then transition into the most critical component of the speech, the thesis statement. We will talk in much greater detail about how to compose an introduction in Chapter 7.

- **A thesis statement.** The thesis statement details the purpose of the speech and articulates the specific issues you will discuss. For instance, your speech's thesis might be, "In order to more fully appreciate the art of pony grooming, we will discuss the history of equine grooming and the proper pony-petting techniques."

- **Main ideas.** Main ideas are key features of any speech; they serve as the backbone of your presentation. Based on your research, you present a few clearly delineated ideas to your audience. Your main ideas should directly contribute to and "link back" to your thesis. In our example, our two main ideas are "the history of equine grooming" and "proper pony-petting techniques."

- **A conclusion.** The conclusion reminds the audience of what they have learned during the speech and usually contains elements (like the AGD) addressed in the introduction. Think of the introduction and the conclusion as matching bookends of your speech.

By now you probably have many questions. What should my introduction sound like? How many points should my speech have? How do I transition between each point? These are all great questions and we will answer most of them in the next few chapters. For now, know that your speech will have a purpose, an introduction, a thesis, main ideas, and a conclusion. You know you have great ideas, you have a sense of how to structure them, and soon you will put those ideas into words.

Adapting Your Writing for a Listening Audience

Structuring your speech will go a long way toward communicating effectively with your audience. In addition to being clearly structured, though, your speech must be clearly written. To best accomplish this, remember the three C's: Clear, Concise, and Coherent.

CLEAR WRITING

Clear writers say exactly what they mean, they say it early, and they say it often. Clear writing has several characteristics:

- **Clear writing uses the active, not passive, voice.** Active voice means that the subject of a sentence is engaged in some sort of action. For instance, the sentence "I kick the ball" begins with the subject "I," who is doing an action, "kicking." A passive form of this sentence would be "The ball is kicked by me." The subject of this sentence, "the ball," is not the actor of the sentence; it is not doing anything.

  Consider the following passages. Can you tell which one is written in the active voice?

  > A. Peanut butter and jelly sandwiches are eaten by me all the time. Every Friday, when I get home from school, the jelly gets taken right out of the refrigerator. Then the peanut butter gets taken out of the cupboard. Eventually, the peanut butter and jelly sandwich gets made and eaten. Peanut

butter and jelly sandwiches are something I enjoy all the time.

B. I love to eat peanut butter and jelly sandwiches. Every Friday, when I get home from school, I go straight to the refrigerator and take out the jelly. Then I go to the cupboard and take out the peanut butter. I make the sandwich, spreading the peanut butter on the bread first, followed by the jelly. I always eat PB&J on Friday, because it is my favorite.

If you chose B, well done. Notice how the active voice engages the reader, creating momentum and suspense. By contrast, the passage using the passive voice is markedly awkward. General audiences often understand the active voice better than the passive.[1] Also, the active voice typically uses fewer words than the passive voice, contributing to concise writing.

- **Clear writers use clear taglines at the beginning of each idea.** Every idea should begin a new paragraph, and each paragraph should begin with a tagline, also called a claim or a topic sentence. The topic sentence of this paragraph is what you just read. Here are two examples of a topic sentence:

   Alexander the Great was an effective leader.

   Government surveillance of citizens degrades public trust.

These topic sentences clearly establish what the ensuing paragraphs will be about, and they are short and to the point. A topic sentence should give the audience a bite-sized piece of information that they can easily manage and understand. Using a topic sentence has two benefits.

First, solid taglines provide immediate satisfaction to the audience. Audiences don't want to work to understand a speech; they are more likely to lose focus if the speaker doesn't make her point early in each paragraph.[2]

Second, solid taglines provide the audience with frameworks that will help them process what follows. Psychologist Jean Piaget used the word "schema" for this sort of framework. Piaget found that the brain processes new information by using existing frames of reference; when we encounter a new object, for instance, the brain compares that object to other objects with which we are already familiar.[3]

If a speaker presents ideas in a speech that may be new or unfamiliar, the audience may struggle to understand them. As speakers, we want to alleviate this struggle. We can help the audience by giving them a useful tagline, or schema, ahead of time. Consider this example from a website about DNA:

> Most prokaryotes lack histones, but they do have supercoiled forms of their DNA held together by special proteins.

Unless you're a biologist, this sentence is probably confusing. What is important in this sentence? What is it about? What on earth are histones? It's not just that the language is technical and confusing, it's that we, as an audience, aren't sure what (or why) we are reading. Now, let's add in the tagline to this paragraph:

> DNA can be further compressed through a twisting process called supercoiling. Most prokaryotes lack histones, but they do have supercoiled forms of their DNA held together by special proteins.

This is probably still a little confusing, but now we at least have a better idea what we are reading; the tagline alerts the audience that what follows is a description of super-coiling. A topic sentence makes it easier for the audience to focus on the most important information in the paragraph.

- **Clear writers use simple language when possible.** Using complicated or obscure words can be disastrous in a speech. Simple language is easier to understand (so the audience is more likely to follow along) and often more powerful (so the audience is more likely to care). The Gettysburg Address, one of the most famous speeches ever given, consists almost entirely of common one- and two-syllable words, as this excerpt illustrates.

> It is rather for us to be here dedicated to the great task remaining before us—that from these hon-ored dead we take increased devotion to that cause for which they gave the last full measure of devotion—that we here highly resolve that these dead shall not have died in vain—that this nation, under God, shall have a new birth of freedom— and that government of the people, by the people, for the people, shall not perish from the earth.

Now consider the following two sentences. Read them silently first. Then read them aloud.

> If you exhibit only a modicum of the extraordi-nary talent you behold, then certainly you will discover success.

> If you use just a little bit of your extraordinary talent, then you will succeed.

Both sentences are easy to understand, but the revision works better in speech. Why? Because words such as "modicum" in the first example make the audience work harder.

- **Clear writers illustrate their ideas, making them as tangible as possible.** Taglines are important because they give an audience a head start on understanding the speaker's ideas, but audiences still may need some extra help. Just like a picture in a science book helps you understand what mitochondria look like, verbal illustrations can help audiences understand complicated concepts. Let's illustrate this with our complicated DNA passage.

> DNA can be further compressed through a twisting process called supercoiling. Most prokaryotes lack histones, but they do have supercoiled forms of their DNA held together by special proteins. Imagine that each DNA strand is a piece of colored string, and you want to use each piece of colored string to make a bracelet for your best friend. You would twist the different colors of string in a pattern, and the more you twist the string, the tighter the bond would be. Finally, your string would not look like the original colored string at all, as all of it twisted together would look like a bracelet. You would tie knots in the end to bind everything together. This is kind of what supercoiling is like. And just like bracelets, supercoils can twist into a myriad of patterns and shapes.

An illustration is a good idea whenever you are trying to describe something complex; it is an especially good idea when you are describing a complex idea in a speech. The stronger the images you create, and the more accessible these images are, the more memorable and impactful your speech will be.

CONCISE WRITING

Concise writers keep sentences short. They know that audiences have short attention spans. By delivering information in small packages, they increase the likelihood that the information is received. Concise writing has three hallmarks.

1. **Concise writing is succinct.** As a speaker, you are speaking with a purpose. Just as using simple language is important, so is using simple sentence structures, especially when you are first presenting an idea. Think of the audience as a small child that doesn't want to eat broccoli. You have to spoon-feed them little, digestible morsels. Short, simple sentences build trust with the audience; easy-to-understand ideas make the audience feel good, because they are able to follow along. Remember that no matter how often you have rehearsed or delivered a speech, the audience will be hearing it for the very first time, so you should make every effort to keep things simple.

2. **Concise writing uses punctuation to enhance organization.** Long sentences can be difficult for an audience to follow because they are dealing with so many distractions and because giving them too much information at one time without breaking it up into manageable packages can be overwhelming for a person to follow while. . .are you still with us? Although a reader might be able to follow that sentence, its lack of punctuation makes it confusing. Using punctuation, to break up sentences or to expand them, is useful in two ways. It helps the speaker separate ideas from one another, and it helps the audience follow a string of ideas.

   Punctuation also helps with breathing. Remember that you will have to say the words you write. Commas, periods, semicolons, and colons are all great opportunities to breathe; writing concisely, and using punctuation effectively, helps control your pace as a speaker. We will discuss vocal delivery more in Chapter 10.

3. **Concise writing avoids clichés and crutch phrases.** Avoid using repetitive or predictable phrases. Clichés can make writing seem unoriginal, but they have a worse effect when used in a speech: they make the audience lose concentration. Read the following passage and pick out the clichés. Is there a way to say some of the phrases that would be more original?

> When considering the controversial nature of this topic, we must realize that a rose by any other name would smell as sweet. Before we all abandon ship, we must ask ourselves, "What's in a name?" I know what you're thinking, he must have an ace up his sleeve. You're thinking that when it comes to this controversy and this speaker, all bets are off. The truth is, I am a man of action, and I burn the candle at both ends. This is the eleventh hour, and we must make a decision. I'm asking you to make a stand for what's right. There is no need to beat your heads against the wall. I promise, I will not ask you to bite off more than you can chew. We can blow the whistle on big government together. Do you trust me?

The ultimate example of concise writing is the Japanese poetry form Haiku, which allows the poet only seventeen syllables to communicate an idea. These poets are masters of word choice, which in public speaking is also called diction. As public speakers, we must be masters of diction. The speaker must make every word count; each word that a speaker chooses is important for achieving her purpose.

Also, public speakers are typically performing under a time limit, so concise writing is imperative.

Let's use the topic of peanut butter and jelly again to practice concise writing. Write out directions for making a peanut butter and jelly sandwich. Then, rewrite the directions using only 25 words. (Hint: use punctuation to help with organization, but don't cheat by omitting necessary speech elements like verbs). Below are a few examples of what we came up with:

Public Speaking Book Writer A:

First, spread peanut butter onto one slice of bread. Then, spread jelly onto the other slice. Put the two slices together and cut in half.

Public Speaking Book Writer B:

Lay two slices of bread on a counter. Spread a desired amount of peanut butter and jelly evenly on each side. Then, fold and eat.

Public Speaking Book Writer C:

Put peanut butter on some bread. Put jelly on some other bread. Put the bread together. Cut the bread with a bread knife.

COHERENT WRITING

Coherent writers make sure all of their ideas connect to one another. They use the natural listening tendencies of audiences to build momentum from one idea to the next, rewarding the audience's expectations. Coherent writing has the following characteristics:

- **Coherent writing works with the audience's expectations.** Taglines should be short and to the point; audience members should be able to understand the tagline and predict what information will come next. Let's revisit the tagline on Alexander the Great. The claim "Alexander the Great was an effective leader" clearly establishes that this paragraph will be about Alexander the Great's qualities as a leader. When presented with a tagline such as this, the audience may naturally ask "Why?" A coherent writer anticipates these questions and provides immediate answers. The next sentence in the paragraph answers this question: "He was an effective leader because he trusted his men, and they trusted him."

- **Coherent writing organizes ideas to serve an overarching purpose.** Coherent writing always focuses on the purpose of the speech, which, as discussed earlier, is both internal and external; the speaker wants to communicate a thesis, and the speaker wants to relate that thesis to the audience. You want to make sure every main idea relates to that core purpose and that core purpose is relevant to your audience. The best place to establish these links is at the end of each idea.

In a full paragraph about Alexander the Great, the last sentence will link the idea explored (Alexander was an effective leader) to the main idea expressed in the thesis (Alexander was an important historical figure):

> Alexander the Great was an effective leader because he trusted his men, and his men trusted him. Once, when Alexander's army was crossing a desert and had only one cup of water left, Alexander poured the water out onto the sand, saying "If there's not enough water for all of my men,

then I won't drink any myself." This showed how close he was to his soldiers, and they respected him for it. *This respect and loyalty enabled him to conquer most of Asia, which was an important historical event.*

This last sentence is sometimes called an impact (because it links the point of the paragraph to the main idea) or an "on-top"[4] (because it connects the idea to what is "on-top" of the speech, the thesis). Relating your ideas to the core purpose of your speech not only helps the audience better understand the ideas of the speech, but also increases the likelihood that the audience will remember the speech because it reinforces each idea with previously learned information.

Relating the idea to the thesis is only part of the task for the speaker, though. The speech must relate not only to itself, but also to its audience. Here is an additional sentence to our Alexander the Great example that serves that purpose:

> These qualities teach us that trust is essential for leadership, even in our modern world.

This two-fold impact makes the speech tighter; each idea relates clearly to the thesis and to the audience. This measure of coherency is important for a listening audience because without it the audience is prone to lose interest.

- **Coherent writing uses previews and reviews.** Any distraction, however miniscule or menacing, can make an audience restless. Fortunately, the speaker is armed with two important tools to ward off such anxiety: the preview and review. Think of your preview as the Welcome! sign to your communicative goal. It helps an audience understand what is coming up and that helps them relax. People love to know what's next. Think of your review as a last-minute reassurance. It helps the audience feel confident that they understood your message. People love to feel confident.

- **Coherent writing uses retrospective and prospective transitions.** When listening to a speech, an audience may ask of the speaker "Where are you going, where have you been?" Consider the signage on U.S. interstate highways. As you drive west through the southeastern United States, you will see signs such as, "You are now leaving Mississippi," and "Welcome to Louisiana." The signs mark the absolute transition between the states through which you are traveling. Similarly, you can use retrospective transitions (which look backward to what was just covered) and prospective transitions (which look forward to what you will cover next) to mark the absolute transitions in your speech. These transitions are referred to as *signposts*.

Signposts tell the audience what was just discussed and prepare them for what is coming up. For example, "Now that I have shared with you why I love peanut butter and jelly sandwiches, I'm going to explain to you how to construct one of these delectable creations." Letting the audience know where you are in your speech helps ease any anxiety they may experience about getting lost among all your words. Signposting also works as a calibration tool. If you lose some of your audience along the way, your retrospective and prospective transitions will help them catch up and follow along. Your signposts will help everyone to refocus together. And your transitions will help take separate ideas and connect them into one coherent message.

Chancelier "xero" Skidmore
Executive Director of Forward Arts, Inc.

In addition to running a non-profit organization that promotes spoken word art forms as a tool for advocacy, Chancelier is the 2014 Individual World Poetry Slam Champion. He is also a published page poet, so he understands that writing for the page and writing for the stage are two different animals.

Like everyone else, I use public speaking as soon as I leave my house in the morning, which is where I guess all the private speaking happens. Today, I performed for cameras. It was a commercial to get former residents to move back to Louisiana. Last week I was teaching a summer camp at Lousiania State University, trying to get a handful of young people to fall in love with poetry.

I use and have used public speaking to elevate my social status, financial status, intellectual status, romantic status, and my status updates.

At the end of the day, it's all about improving where we are in the world. That can be achieved by elevating the world, but it can also be achieved by elevating oneself. I'd like to think I regularly attempt both.

As a teacher, I instruct my students that the study of language is and will always be the most important of all their classes. People rarely make a great first impression in a job interview or on a first date with a math equation. If people cannot communicate in this society, they cannot participate in this society. They cannot compete and often they cannot survive. Other courses are important. And we use spoken and written language to study them, as well."

I performed a poem about George Stinney for a state juvenile justice convention. George Stinney is the youngest person to ever be executed by the United States judicial system. I felt like I was speaking to the very people who could do something about the way young African Americans are vilified at an early age and put on the path to prison by a biased society.

Simplicity works very well on stage. On the page, the writer knows her readers have the luxury of languishing within the lines of every stanza, pondering one image before casually drifting on to the next. On stage, poems happen in real time. A certain level of complexity can be achieved, but the spoken word writer must never forget that the listening audience cannot pause or rewind a performance. If the spoken word writer yearns to be successful within the realm of that genre, the collective sophistication of the room often has to be taken into account.

Ultimately, the mastery of your craft is all you have control over. Audiences are fickle, and speakers never can tell exactly why they are embraced or shunned by the masses. My advice is to decide what you'd be comfortable failing at and then do your damnedest to not fail. Who knows? Your audience might decide to like you. If not, at least you like yourself.

A Note About Tone and Your Personal Voice

When you write for a listening audience, you should be clear, concise, and coherent, but you should not deny your own voice. You have the ability to deliver your message in a way that no other person can. The language choices, like using formal or informal language, contractions, pop culture references, all contribute to the *tone* of a speech. President George W. Bush would often use colloquial language in his speeches, which supported his cowboy image and folksy attitude. President Barack Obama has a tendency to package his speech into short, easily digestible phrases to communicate in a way that conveys directness and efficiency.

Now, do not fret if you do not know what your unique style or voice is. Trust us, it's there. It is in the way that you say certain words or phrase certain ideas. Maybe you say, "What a deal!" every time you hear good news. Maybe you use contractions or maybe you never touch them. These idiosyncrasies compose your voice, and your voice will grow and mature as you become more experienced with writing for a listening audience.

Tying It Together: Authentic Communication

You will write a speech for an American History presentation with a tone that's different from the one you give to pump up the student body before a football game. Although we strongly believe that following the guidelines laid out in this chapter is the best way to communicate when speaking, we realize that they are guidelines, not laws, and we recognize that the very best writers often deviate from guidelines and rules.

Clear and concise writing is a great starting place for a speech, but sometimes you need a little something extra. Sometimes making a peanut butter and jelly sandwich will take more than 25 words; sometimes Alexander the Great is a spectacular leader, not just an effective one. You can use other sources to help you develop your personal style and tone further. (Strunk and White's *Elements of Style*, Stephen King's *On Writing*, and Graff and Birkenstein's *They Say, I Say* are our personal suggestions.) For now, though, focus on implementing the ideas in this chapter. If you do, you will communicate effectively for every listening audience.

Writing Things People Hear

Below is an adapted excerpt from a movie review. Use the excerpts to build a six-sentence speech. For each sentence (1–6), read the three choices out loud, then choose which excerpt (A, B, or C) best represents text written for a listening audience. Compile your choices into your six-sentence speech and deliver it with supreme confidence to an audience member of your choosing. Mix and match to try to build the perfect speech written for a listening audience. The suggested order is located at the bottom of the chart.

	A	B	C
1.	I'm not someone who derives satisfaction from solving a movie's plot before the movie solves it for me.	I don't like to guess a movie's plot ahead of time.	Guessing the plot of a movie before the movie solves it for me does not generally make me happy.
2.	I want to get the surprise that I paid for.	I'm paying for the satisfaction of surprise.	I am shelling out my cash to get taken for a thrill ride of surprising narrative and suspense.
3.	I am looking for a movie to poke fun at my feeble attempts at being clever by pulling the rug out from under me when I least expect it.	What I want from a movie is to make fun of my attempts to figure things out and then twist things around.	I'm paying for a movie to mock my sense of cleverness or compound it with some cleverness of its own.

4.	You're always five scenes ahead of *Getaway*, and it's exasperating.	I was really frustrated when I saw *Getaway* and I was able to guess what was going to happen way ahead of time.	When you watch the movie *Getaway*, you never get what you pay for because you are always able to guess what happens before it happens, and it's exhausting.
5.	Europeans have forcibly imprisoned the wife of a former racecar driver, who has undergone traumatic events. The men who took the wife force the driver to steal a high-tech Mustang and drive it around to cause ultimate destruction.	Euro-baddies have kidnapped the wife of a traumatized former racecar driver and commanded him, by cell phone, to steal a Mustang rigged with surveillance cameras and drive it around Bulgaria in a way that causes maximum chaos.	European bad guys kidnapped a retired racecar driver's wife and forced the guy to steal a car and drive it around Bulgaria in order to cause mass chaos.
6.	If he refuses, they'll kill her.	If he fails to submit to their commands, they will annihilate her.	If he say's no, they'll kill her.

Suggested Order: b, a, b, c, c, b

*Source text from "License to Bore," by Wesley Morris. First featured in GRANTLAND August 29, 2013.

Key Concepts

- Listening audiences have a more difficult time overcoming internal and external interference.

- Every speech will have a purpose, a thesis, an introduction, some main points, and a conclusion.

- Writing for a listening audience should be clear, concise, and coherent.

- Clear writing uses active, simple, and tangible language.

- Concise writing is brief, uses punctuation effectively, and avoids clichés.

- Coherent writing meets audience expectations and ties ideas together with previews, reviews, and transitions.

CHAPTER 5

Topic Selection

Jean Buridan, a 14th-century French philosopher, wrote that if a person is faced with two equally good options, he would be unable to choose between them and so would do nothing. This decision (or lack thereof) is satirized by a paradox known as "Buridan's Ass"; a donkey, faced with two equally tasty piles of hay, cannot choose between them, and so starves to death.

Speakers often have to choose very specific topics to meet the demands of the situation or audience, but even when given complete freedom to choose, they often struggle to come up with a topic that fits their purpose and will register with their audience. When confronted with the task of topic selection, speakers often feel like Buridan's Ass.

In this chapter you will learn to solve your topic dilemma. This chapter will help you analyze your speech's purpose, select a focused topic, and then craft an effective thesis statement.

What Are We All Doing Here, Anyway?

Understanding the context of your speech will go a long way toward determining your topic. The context includes the speech and the audience's reaction, and it also includes the purpose of the speech. The event could be anything: a presentation in your public speaking class, a public meeting at city hall, or a roast of Kevin Costner.

Several factors define a public speaking event and help you understand the context of your speech:

- **Occasion.** Speeches typically take place during a specific occasion—a party, a funeral, a class. The nature of the occasion can help narrow the range for your topic. If the occasion will be festive, then a serious, somber topic might not be appropriate; if the event will be somber, then a speech about cute kittens may not be ideal.

- **Venue.** The venue is the physical space where the speech will occur, and it can affect your topic selection in interesting ways. If you are speaking in a church, for instance, you will probably have a different range of topics than if you were speaking in a nightclub. In this way, a venue may restrict the topics you select, but it can also *suggest* topics. If you are delivering a speech to the Parent Teacher Association in a classroom, you may consider talking about classroom instruction; the same speech delivered in an auditorium or a cafeteria may not have as much impact. The venue provides much of the context of an event, and so when selecting topics you should be working with the nature of the venue, not against it.

- **Assignment.** Assignments don't end when you graduate; they happen at many types of events. You may be asked to deliver a commencement address or to present the specifications of a new product to a client. Obviously, if you have a specific assignment, it will provide some guidance for your selection of a topic. Keep in mind, though, that even when given an assignment, you will still need to make choices about how to focus on a specific idea. We'll cover that later in this chapter.

- **Time of day.** If you will be presenting your ideas during or right after a meal, you may want to avoid topics that could disrupt your audience's appetite. Speeches delivered early in the morning might require a certain level of energy to keep your audience awake.

- **Program.** It is important to know what the event's program will be. If others will be speaking, their topics may influence your selection. Also consider what other activities your audience might engage in during the event, for example, eating, playing basketball, or listening to a concert. The schedule of events can inform your topic selection so that you are working with context and not against it.

Why Am I Talking, Why Are You Listening?

Once you have a better understanding of the event, you can identify the **purpose** of the speech. In Chapter 1, we divided purposes into two broad categories: internal and external. Internal purposes relate to the speaker's personal goals for the speech, while external purposes relate to the audience experience the speaker wants to create. Your internal purposes are your own, and when they are clear, your topic selection process will often be very simple. External purposes vary more widely, though, so we'll briefly address some of the more common external purposes and how they may affect your topic selection.

SPEAKING TO PERSUADE

A speaker taking the stage to persuade is a very common public speaking event. Sometimes the occasion will call for persuasion, as in a debate or a town hall meeting. Other times, the occasion will be more neutral, but someone or some event may provide a particular persuasive assignment for the speaker, for example, you may be able to persuade your fellow survivors in the lifeboat not to eat all the food at once. Whatever the reason, consider two questions when selecting your topic for a persuasive speech.

1. **What is important to you?** *Passion is a prerequisite to persuasion.* So, when preparing a persuasive speech, first determine what you care about. We have seen countless persuasive speeches derailed because the speaker had little or no personal investment in the subject matter. If you are not enthusiastic about what you are saying, why should your audience be? Create a list of topics that you consider important, and then stay within that list when choosing your topic.

   In some cases, you may not be able to choose a topic you care deeply about, but even in these circumstances you could find something about the topic to which you can commit. You may not find tax policy exciting, but if you can connect tax policy to a topic you care about, like education, you may be able to find the passion you need to persuade.

2. **What is important to your audience?** We will discuss how to analyze your audience more thoroughly in Chapter 11, but knowing your audience bears on our task here as well. Understanding what is important to them can help you in two different ways.

First, it might help you choose a topic that the audience already cares about, so the audience will be excited to listen to the speech. If you are speaking at a rally for a teacher's union, you might be able to persuade the audience to vote for a political candidate by emphasizing her support for public education. If you are speaking to a class of high school students, you might choose to talk about extracurricular activities that they might enjoy.

Second, knowing what your audience cares about may lead you to select a topic that is outside their comfort zone. Thinking about that same class of high school students, you may choose to talk about community service specifically because you know that this group of students *doesn't* particularly care about volunteering, and you think it's important to change their minds. Either way, understanding what is important to your audience can play a major role in choosing your topic.

SPEAKING TO INFORM

Another common speaking purpose is to inform. Once again, the context of the speech may determine the purpose: a speaker may be delivering a lecture on how to use new technology or reporting on a current event. When choosing a topic for this type of speech, you can use a process similar to the one for developing a persuasive topic.

- **What do you know?** Just as with persuasive speaking, informative speeches are best when the speaker is invested in the subject matter. Caring deeply about the material is still important, but for informative speaking, the speaker must also deeply understand the material. That is not to say that you will know everything about every topic you might choose, but taking inventory of your knowledge base can help you select a topic. You might end up choosing a topic about which you are already an expert, or you may choose one about which you want to learn more. The former tends to be a bit easier, but both can be effective strategies.

- **What does the audience know?** Even if our audience knows very little, you can use their interests and possible knowledge base as a guide for selecting a topic. And, as with persuasive speaking, you can do so in different ways. You can select a topic that the audience is already comfortable with, knowing that they may be more interested as a result or maybe just more able to follow along. Alternatively, you can select a topic about which the audience knows relatively little, hoping to broaden their horizons with new information. Again, considering the audience's perspective is important as you sort through potential topics.

A Storm is Coming—A BRAINstorm!

Once you have a sense of the event and the purpose of your speech, you will be better equipped to begin choosing a topic. The selection process should start with brainstorming topics.

Begin with what you know. In fact, Tammy Miller of Toastmasters International writes, "The best place to start looking for a speech topic is in the mirror. What information do you already know? What can you share about your life that others will find interesting?"[1]

But what does that mean? It means answering questions such these:

Brainstorming: The Question Way

- What do you know about?

- What do you love?

- What does the audience know about?

- What does the audience love?

- What does the audience need to know?

- What does the audience want to know?

- What should your audience want to know? Why?

- What is happening in the news that strikes your interest?

- What is trending in social media?

After the initial brainstorm, you are ready to narrow your subject into a refined topic. You can do so in several ways.

- **Gravitate to your interests.** A great way to narrow your topic is to choose aspects of a subject that you find particularly interesting. For example, if you were to speak about giraffes, you would address what interests you most about giraffes. What has always fascinated you about them? The unique spot patterns? The long necks? Protecting them?

- **Choose topics you have stories about.** Choosing topics based on the stories you know is another way of mining your own experiences to focus on a topic. We are born as storytellers and we intuitively use storytelling to support our opinions and interests. If you have unique experiences (or have relationships with people who have unique experiences) that support a cause that is important to you—like human rights, the dangers of alcohol abuse, cancer treatment and awareness, college readiness, patriotism, or cultural diversity—you should choose a topic that capitalizes on these experiences. Not only will you find crafting your speech easier, but your speech will likely have a deeper impact, as well.

- **Check the news.** If you have difficulty choosing between two topics, follow the lead of journalists, who determine which stories to pursue by considering their newsworthiness. They keep in mind the significance, proximity, prominence, and most important, the timing of the story.[2] People read, watch, or listen to the news to learn about events that will affect them now or in the future. If an important city council meeting happened yesterday, we want to know how the information from that meeting will affect us.

Timing is everything in news; it is also important when considering a topic. If you choose to speak out against what you think is a terrible law, make sure the law is still on the books. Some topics, particularly those involving problems well suited for persuasive speeches, may already have been solved. If you are delivering an informative speech, you want to make sure the information is new to your audience.

So how do you find timely topics? Read through science magazines like *Popular Science*, *Scientific American*, or *Psychology Today*. Browse tech blogs like io9.com and gizmodo.com. When an article piques your interest, dig a little deeper. Read the journal publication or the study that the article is reporting on for more complete information. Browse your local paper to find issues that are important within your community. When you read with your speaking event in mind, you can better determine whether or not the information is appropriate.

If you practice becoming a more informed person, more often than not the topic will find you. As collegiate speech coaches, we have to practice sorting the news we consume. When we hear a radio story about an interesting new technology that will help farmers grow crops in difficult terrain, we file that away as a potential topic for an informative speech. If a friend sends us an email to sign a petition to improve conditions for domestic workers, we file that away as a potential topic for a persuasive speech. Be on the lookout; speech topics are everywhere if you are paying attention.

Adrian Uribarri
Communications Strategist

Adrian is an urban adventurer at heart. He has worked in newspapers, radio stations, and classrooms in California, Florida, Illinois, and now New York. His experience across communications platforms means he is never at a loss for words, and his current job is to use those words, both spoken and written, to help people and organizations explain ideas and persuade others. Adrian suggests that you are not ready to begin writing your speech until you are able to make your point in one sentence.

Speaking clearly and persuasively is crucial when I'm presenting to clients, participating on a panel at a professional conference, or explaining a complex strategy to someone outside of my field.

Having firsthand experience as a public speaker helps me coach my clients more effectively and give them the confidence they need to reach and influence their audiences.

It's easier to make friends when you're comfortable talking with strangers.

One of my teachers said that people will judge you based on how you speak and how you write. That's not always true, but it's true enough.

Language transfers meaning, and meaningful ideas are valuable. The more effectively we can use language, the more value we bring to others' lives.

Speech is more dynamic than the written word. To speak well, particularly in conversation, requires improvisation. Speaking clearly and persuasively, in the moment, is a rare and coveted skill.

I traveled to Latin America on grants from the U.S. State Department to give talks on journalism ethics and digital media to audiences in Colombia, El Salvador, and Guatemala. Those are great memories because I was able to talk about my profession in Spanish, the language of my ancestors, and to professionals and students who don't have the range of opportunities that I do in the United States.

Even in black and white and two dimensions, watching Martin Luther King Jr.'s "I Have a Dream" speech stirs me so deeply. As someone who grew up in the 1990s and became politically conscious in the 2000s, I'm not sure there's a contemporary equivalent.

Make your point in one sentence. If you can't do that, then you're probably not ready to write the rest of the speech.

If you think your idea is too big and complicated to break down this way, then it's probably even more important that you do.

Distilling simplicity from complexity is an act of intellectual discipline and strength. It's also an act of service to your audience.

We Need a Little Focus in Our Lives (and Speech Topics)

If your topic is too broad, the audience has a hard time figuring out what they are supposed to do with the information. So, craft a focused topic by considering what sub-topics might exist within your topic. We were once asked to write a lecture about "Goals," which struck us as a very broad topic. So we brainstormed and asked, "What do we know about goals?" and "What does the audience need to know about goals?" Our efforts generated sub-topics that fit within the larger topic: How to Set Goals, How to Achieve Goals, Why are Goals Important, and Short-term vs. Long-term Goals. We chose one of our sub-topics (How to Set Achievable Goals) and then wrote a riveting lecture.

WRITING A GREAT THESIS

Once you have narrowed down your topic, you must determine your thesis, then gather supporting ideas to create a great speech. At a minimum, the thesis should clearly express your reason for communicating with the audience. Note that the thesis statement should be more than just restating your narrow topic. If your topic is "String Cheese," then the thesis would not be "Hey, let me tell you about string cheese." A more appropriate thesis might be, "String cheese is a delicious, healthy, and simple snack, and you should eat more of it." The second option conveys a purpose for the speech: to explain the benefits of snacking on string cheese.

Using the thesis as a way to communicate the purpose of your speech is all fine and dandy, but to present a great thesis statement you must use it to convince the audience that your speech is important. A more complex thesis statement alerts the audience to listen.

For a stronger thesis, begin with a "because" statement. Consider these examples:

> Because trees are the backbone of the global eco-system, we must understand the threats facing trees today.

> Because everyone likes to snack, we should all eat healthy, delicious string cheese.

A "because" statement forces you to put your justification for your thesis into words, and can win the audience over before you've even begun your argument. And if you're delivering an informative speech, it can strongly communicate a reason to listen. The "because" statement says, "Listen up. This matters."

Consider our thesis statement about goals:

> Because goals determine the direction for which you are preparing, and because confidence should be nurtured and protected, the goals you set must be achievable and manageable.

We justified the speech while making it clear to the audience what was to come.

Keep in Mind, You Can Always Change Yours

Researching and preparing for a speech can sometimes challenge our frame of reference, or the way we see the world. Our ethnicity, our religious background, our gender identity, our experiences, and our upbringing make up our frame of reference, which is activated when we brainstorm speech topics. Our interest in a certain informative topic or our passion for a given persuasive topic is a result of our frame of reference.

But sometimes our frame of reference may be based on incomplete or inaccurate information. For example, you might have heard that the Great Chicago Fire of 1871 was caused by a cow kicking over a lantern while Mrs. O'Leary was milking it. You loved this story, and you were eager to share it with your classmates in a speech entitled "How a Clumsy Cow Changed Chicago." Once you did a little research, though, you realized that what you heard was wrong. While the fire likely originated on the O'Leary farm, the journalist who first reported the story confessed that he made the cow part up. Everything you thought you knew about the Great Chicago Fire of 1871 was a lie!

When honing in on your specific topic, you may realize that you were misled by your frame of reference. Don't panic. Part of the research process is learning something you didn't know before. When you discover that what you thought you knew was wrong, you can and should change your mind. Don't be afraid to do so; it's all part of the process.

Tying It Together: Authentic Communication

Every person or book that has ever offered advice on public speaking, from the legendary Toastmasters to *Public Speaking for Dummies*, has encouraged presenters to speak on subjects that they care about. Why do so many experts offer the same advice? Because your topic has to matter to you for it to matter to your audience.

In any given speech, you are responsible for being true to three parties: your topic, your audience, and yourself. In persuasive speeches, you are charged with picking a side and defending a position. Your position will, or at the very least can, affect people. There is a great responsibility in this possibility. In your informative speech, you have a responsibility to be accurate with how the information is packaged and presented.

In all public speaking events, you have a responsibility to be truthful to your audience. Finally, you have a responsibility to yourself. Whether you believe in what you are saying or not, your audience will always *assume* that you do. Consequently, what you say in your speeches is a reflection of your values, attitudes, and beliefs. Authentic communication involves the understanding that what you say represents your ideological values and worldview. In short, you have many ways to arrive at a topic, but it starts, and ends, with you.

LET'S GIVE A SPEECH

Choose Your Own Speaking Adventure

Because we want you to select some wonderful future topics for some fantastic future speeches, we are going to lead you through the selection process, before we have you speak about your adventure.

Your Mission

Princess Persuasion is trapped in a cave that is guarded by the powerfully minded and well-read Conversation Dragon. Many have tried to save the princess from Conversation Dragon's talons, but they have all been shrouded by his wit and devoured by his flame of convolution. Conversation Dragon has one weakness: Good Speech Topics. Follow the path to exciting speech topics below to save Princess Persuasion.

OCCASION	VENUE	AUDIENCE
The rescue of the princess	The mouth of a cave in an undisclosed mythical location	A fire-breathing dragon who reads and reasons

Step 1: Choose a Purpose.

☐ TO INFORM   ☐ TO PERSUADE

Step 2: Brainstorm.
Choose one answer for each question.

If you choose **TO INFORM …**	If you choose **TO PERSUADE …**

1. What do you know about the dragon?

    ☐ He breathes fire

    ☐ He likes to read

2. What do you love about the princess?

    ☐ She is rich

    ☐ She is persuasive

3. What does the dragon need to know about the princess?

    ☐ She is a champion archer

    ☐ She also likes to read

4. What is happening in the news that strikes your interest?

    ☐ War

    ☐ Celebrities naming babies crazy things.

1. What does the dragon know about?

    ☐ Fire-breathing

    ☐ Killing potential rescuers

2. What does the dragon love?

    ☐ Books

    ☐ Other dragons

3. What does the dragon want to know about the princess?

    ☐ Is her family rich?

    ☐ Does she taste like chicken?

4. What should the dragon know about the princess?

    ☐ Does she feel pain?

    ☐ What are some of her favorite hobbies?

5. What is trending in social media?	5. What is trending in social media?
☐ Pop-star says something stupid	☐ Pop-star says something stupid

Step 3: Write A Thesis.

Using the template, compose a compelling thesis for your speech.

TO INFORM	TO PERSUADE
Because [insert reason that the Conversation Dragon should be informed of your topic], you should consider [insert topic] and release Princess Persuasion from captivity.	Because [insert reason that the Conversation Dragon should be persuaded by your topic], you should consider [insert topic] and release Princess Persuasion from captivity.

Step 4: Memorize and Perform.
Stand before the Conversation Dragon and deliver your thesis with confidence. Feel free to repeat the process and marvel at the topics that you can generate.

Key Concepts

- Public speaking events have several components: an occasion, a venue, an assignment, a time of day, and a program.

- When selecting a topic, consider your interests and the interests of your audience.

- You can narrow your topic by considering your interests, thinking about stories and narratives, and focusing on newsworthy ideas.

- Thesis statements should convince your audience to listen to the rest of your speech.

- It's never too late to change your mind (or the focus of your speech).

CHAPTER 6

Research

Over time, with new technologies and social norms, more and more of the world's information has become available to more and more people. Information is produced, distributed, and stored across a great variety of mediums: books, the telephone, newspapers, magazines, journals, radio, television. People can hear, read, or witness information about the world around them and then share it with others, instantly. Modern technologies only accelerate this production and reproduction of information.

With all the information that is out there, we must work hard to prepare for our own contribution to the world's ever-growing store. And that's where research comes in. Research empowers us to contribute with confidence and also is the key that unlocks the world around us. Great research is a prerequisite to a great speech. This chapter will help you plan, conduct, organize, and incorporate your research into your speech.

Selecting a Topic Through Research

So, theoretically, you've already selected a topic. The previous chapter discussed various strategies and approaches for topic selection, and we think it was pretty helpful. But if you're still looking for a topic, this chapter will give you an even stronger chance of finding or developing one; everything we say about research here is designed to help you prepare for your speech, but could just as easily be applied to the process of researching to find a topic in the first place.

Why Research?

We research before we speak in public for many reasons.

- **We research to learn and grow.** We established in Chapter 1 that two of the purposes of public speaking are to learn about the world around us and to grow as individuals. When you research, you have a great opportunity to learn about the world, and you also develop lifelong skills. Many speakers make the mistake of researching within the narrow confines of their speech structure or for the specific purpose of finding support for their individual arguments or points. This strategy limits what they get out of the process. It's like going to a world-class museum, trying to find one specific painting, and refusing to look at anything else you pass. It's a wasted opportunity. When researching, engage your curiosity: follow ideas and be open to learning new things, even if they don't seem directly relevant to your speech.

- **We research to master our material and improve our performance.** Researching beyond the scope of your topic allows you to build confidence through understanding. Let's say you are writing a speech about protecting wild wolf populations and you come across an author who says that wolves must be protected because of territory fragmentation. You could immediately insert that piece of research into your speech and move on to another point, but what exactly is territory fragmentation? What causes it? Why is it so dangerous to wolves? By mastering these related ideas and understanding the concept more deeply, you will be able to more confidently present the idea when you speak. As you learned in Chapter 3, mastering your material helps you remember it. Stronger research makes stronger speakers.

- **We research to improve our speech.** So maybe this one is obvious, but, even if it is, it bears repeating. Remember Aristotle's three forms of persuasion; logos, ethos, and pathos are all enhanced through research. Your logic and arguments will improve if you are writing from a solid foundation of research and understanding; you can also use research to find or illustrate emotional appeals. It is ethos, though, that benefits most from research. When you speak, you have to establish your credibility, and mastering your material through research will help you do that. But let's face it: you will often speak about subjects on which you are not, sadly, an expert. To compensate for this, you must supplement your own perspective with evidence from other sources. You must protect the wolves, you say. "Says who?" replies the audience. "Says every wolf expert in the world," you say. "Fair enough" says the audience.

Sources
Speakers often view researching as a hassle; they imagine sorting through library catalogs, reading through books, or

looking for special academic sources. But this is a very narrow view of what constitutes research. Potential sources for your speech are all around you: newspapers, magazines, movies, TV shows, government reports, radio shows, academic studies, Supreme Court decisions, books—and, of course, the Internet.

Research doesn't have to be confined to one building or one type of source; research happens all the time. What's that you heard someone say on *The Daily Show*? Talk about it in your speech. What's that interesting thing you saw on Reddit? Talk about it in your speech. What's that thing sitting over there? Talk about it in your speech.

Of course, sometimes you can't or shouldn't integrate what's happening around you into your speech. So let's establish some guidelines for seeking out and identifying quality sources.

- **Seek sources that match the purpose, tone, and setting of your speech.** Some speeches, either because they are delivered in a serious setting or because they are about serious topics, may require a more serious level of research. If the speech is about an academic topic, you should cite serious academic sources; if you are trying to entertain your audience, you can use more pop culture references.

- **Seek sources that are credible.** There are many potential sources for every speech, so we don't want you to discount anything out of hand. Remember, though, that one important function of research is to build and supplement your credibility with testimony from trustworthy experts. This is not to say that you should use only academic sources; you should be concerned about the source's relevance or authority in a given field. Using sources that have little authority concerning the topic does more harm than good. When you find sources that are not familiar, investigate them to establish their credentials. Try Googling your source or author, or, on websites, see if the site has an "About" section.

- **Be aware of source bias.** Note that we are not saying to always avoid biased sources, but be aware of the bias that sources might have. Generally, you should prefer objective sources to biased ones, but a biased source isn't necessarily unusable. The Wildlife Conservation Society (WCS) is a biased source because it works explicitly for the conservation of wildlife. But, as a well-respected not-for-profit organization, the WCS is also credible. You could cite the WCS comfortably in your speech, but recognizing the possible bias, you would do well to seek other sources to provide a well-rounded view. If all the sources in a speech have the same clear bias, then you are not building credibility.

- **Prefer recent sources when possible, but especially when discussing current events.** Some types of sources do not need to be current; there are very few breaking news stories about the life of Aristotle. Some information is stable and relatively unaffected by the modern world's comings and goings. Other topics, like the conflict in Syria, require up-to-the-minute information. Using outdated sources can destroy your credibility and reveal that you did not do enough research.

BUT HOW DO I FIND ALL THESE SOURCES?

There are many ways to find sources for your speech, but we suggest that you type what you're looking for into Google. We'll cover some Googling tips later. Here are some other suggestions.

- **Start by getting an overview of your topic.** You should first go to a source that can give you a broad outline, to see what the main issues or points of interest are. Use this initial phase to take notes; think of it as a "map" of your topic. And check out any sources cited that might guide you further. Later, you will decide where you want to take a closer look.

- **Use key terms to refine your search.** Sometimes you will come across some specific terms that academics or experts use in discussing your topic. For instance, experts in the field of political finance may use the term "corporate personhood" to talk about the right of corporations to contribute to political campaigns; similarly, experts in Harry Potter may refer to "legilimency" when discussing the art of reading and controlling minds. Searching on key terms will help you get more precise results that are more likely to be written by experts.

- **Add structural language to your searches.** Add phrases like "arguments for" or "overview of" to your searches to produce helpful articles and sources more quickly.

- **Use the advanced search options to get better results.** If you're looking for recent results, just add the current year or even the current month to your search terms. Also, most academic research and book excerpts published on the Internet are formatted as PDF documents, so if you're looking for more credible sources, search for PDF documents (add "filetype:pdf" to your search). Finally, you can use quotation marks around phrases to produce more specific results. If you want results about the European Union but keep getting results for Gabrielle Union's new European hairstyle, try searching for "European Union"; this will return results that use that exact phrase.

- **Type what you're looking for into Google.** We cannot stress this enough. Our most commonly heard complaint from students conducting research is that they cannot find "x." We always ask them if they typed "x" into Google. They always say they haven't tried that. Here is a helpful chart to illustrate exactly what we mean.

How To Find What You're Looking For Using Google

If You're Looking For . . .	*Type This Into Google*
• Types of trees in North America	• "Types of trees in North America"
• Reasons to legalize marijuana	• "Reasons to legalize marijuana"
• How to make a dinner table	• "How to make a dinner table"
• Why the United States invaded Iraq	• "Why the United States invaded Iraq"
• The benefits of drinking water	• "The benefits of drinking water"

- **Use other tools besides Google.** First, all of these search tips we discussed above will work in any search engine you use. Second, and maybe more important, using Google, you may not be able to access many valuable academic databases such as LexisNexis, JStor, and EbscoHost. Although they can be somewhat more difficult to use and often require paid subscriptions, they are valuable aids for serious research. Consider visiting your local library and asking if they offer access to these (or any other) databases through their systems, and don't forget to ask if a librarian is available to assist you. They love that sort of thing.

CONDUCTING INTERVIEWS

There may be some information that is important to your research but no one else felt was important enough to write down. Who painted the mural in the town square? How many people did it take to wrap up the World's Largest Ball of Twine in your county? What was it like when your town was first desegregated? In these cases, the best way to find the information you need might be by conducting interviews. Here's how.

- **Determine who has the information you need.** One of the great challenges of gathering information through interviews is finding the right person to interview. For example, you may be working on a speech about a supposedly haunted bridge in your hometown. First and foremost, you want to consider who has the information you need. Someone who recently moved to your town might not be the best person to interview since he has never heard of the haunted bridge. Instead, ask a local tour guide.

   You will also want to consider whether or not your interview candidate has ethos, or credibility, to speak on the subject. For example, if you are writing a speech about innovative Hip Hop practices, former vice president Dick

Cheney is a terrible interviewee. Eminem would be better. Similarly, citing your "best friend Pete" in your persuasive speech about tax policy might not be the best idea. Even though Pete is a great guy, he isn't exactly a credible source, so citing him will hurt your credibility too.

- **Ask the right questions to get the information you need.** Now that you have an interview subject who is knowledgeable and credible, determine what questions to ask. You will want to create an "interview protocol," a list of questions that will guide your session. The person you are interviewing is sacrificing her time to help you out, so you don't want to waste any of it. Also, drafting an interview protocol will ensure that you get all the information you need.

  What sort of questions should you ask? Great question! Because great questions are clear, relevant to the subject, and open-ended. Using language like "describe" or "explain" will keep your questions open-ended. Avoid questions to which your subject can answer "yes" or "no"; they will get you very little useful information. Bad questions are unclear or off-topic. Bad questions are those you already know the answer to. If you are only asking a question to guide your interviewee to say what you want to say in the speech, you are asking a bad question.

Good Questions	Bad Questions
CLEAR	**UNCLEAR**
What happens during a typical morning working as the manager for Joe Smith's mayoral campaign?	So what is like to work here?

TOPICAL	NOT TOPICAL
What advice would you give young people who are interested in pursuing a career in public relations?	Whoa, you LIVE here? Awesome!

OPEN-ENDED	CLOSE-ENDED
Describe the experience when you first learned you were receiving the Medal of Honor.	Is that the Medal of Honor on your wall?

UNGUIDED	GUIDED
Explain how you were impacted emotionally when you thought you might lose your job?	Tell me how scared you were when you thought you might lose your job? Would you describe your fear as horrifying or was it more of an absolute terror?

- **Say "thank you."** When someone offers her time for your interview, make sure to thank her for it. You may consider sending her a thank you note or offer to buy her coffee (or do both, actually). It might be a nice gesture to send her a copy or recording of your speech or, even better, invite her to watch your presentation. Do *something* to show you appreciate her participation.

What Do We Do With Research?

So you took our advice to heart and you researched beyond your topic; you engaged your curiosity and learned about the world. You tracked down diverse, credible sources. What's next?

LET'S ORGANIZE THIS PIECE

Organizing your research is important so that the information you've gathered is easily accessible as you construct your speech. Here are some tips for organizing.

- **Use annotation, summary, and synthesis while researching.** Taking a lot of notes as you research will help you organize your material later. Sometimes you may want to jot down notes as you read an online source, but working with physical, print sources is also very helpful. As you're researching, *annotate* your sources. Don't just passively flip through information or sources and assume you will come back to them later. You can use several techniques: you can highlight or underline important information, or you can take notes in the margins. Of course, only do this with sources you've either purchased or printed out for yourself (don't mark up a library book, for instance).

  After you've completely annotated a source, spend some time *summarizing* the information it contains. This will help give you an overview of what material is available, and will reinforce your own learning of the information.

- **Record the source as well as the information.** Don't worry too much about getting all the possible information from each source, or all the possible information *about* each source. Record enough information about the source so you can locate it later. Bookmark the website or note the name of the book and page number if you are researching from a physical manuscript. If your assignment for the speech will require a special citation format (Modern Language Association, American Psychological Association, etc.), you can always come back to the source for the specific information you need later. As you research, keep your focus on learning and organizing your material; don't get bogged down in details yet.

- **Group your sources and information together by main ideas.** As you begin to amass research, think ahead to potential organizational choices for your speech. Make connections between research and group your sources together so you can quickly revisit them as you begin to outline and assemble your speech.

Rana Yared
Managing Director at Goldman Sachs

Rana graduated from the University of Pennsylvania (Go Quakers!) in 2006 and went to work in New York City. She then lived in London for almost five years and earned a masters degree from the London School of Economics. She loves to cook, travel, and take photographs. She also reads the latest books on politics, war, peace, just about everything. Rana claims that there is no substitute for good preparation.

My job challenges me each day to communicate my views logically and succinctly.

Look people in the eye, look happy to be there, and listen carefully.

Each time I speak to an audience of one or one hundred, I go through the same preparation—do I have the facts? What is my point of view or what is the message I want to leave the person or people to whom I am speaking?

Public speaking gives you the confidence to think on your feet and the ability to stand up in a front of a room and account for your point of view.

Perhaps counter intuitively, speaking in public teaches you to listen to others.

These skills are the basic foundation for scholastic excellence in university, survival in a first job, and good leadership thereafter.

Slow down—if others cannot process your message, it is as if it were never said.

I saw Sen. George Mitchell speak at Chatham House a few years ago about the Irish Peace Process and the continued lack of peace in the Middle East. I had expected his comments to be rehearsed, well hedged and oblique. Instead, he came across as warm, sincere, and very direct. He held the entire room at attention, while making the experience feel like a fireside chat. His style was hugely persuasive without overtly giving the impression that he was trying to convince the audience of anything.

I was a shy kid.

Always command your content, whether it is English Literature, foreign policy or finance; there is no substitute for good preparation and conviction.

People will mistake your lack of confidence for lack of knowledge. If you have the knowledge, then you should not lack confidence.

Smile—it makes the whole experience much more pleasant.

CITING SOURCES

Now that you have all your research organized, you will have an easier time organizing and preparing your speech. But you will still need to share this research with others by citing your sources when you speak. You cite sources in a speech for two important reasons.

1. **Citing sources establishes credibility.** We've already mentioned this several times: establishing credibility is one of the fundamental goals of a speaker. By demonstrating that experts agree with your position, or by illustrating your point with timely and appropriate research, you will gain influence over your audience.

   Even if you are not citing experts, you can still earn the interest of your audience by citing interesting research or research with which the audience is familiar. For instance, if we are talking about a complex idea, but illustrate using an episode of *Sesame Street*, the audience will more likely understand—and like—us.

2. **Citing sources helps avoid plagiarism.** Plagiarism is the uncredited use of someone else's words or ideas[1] either intentionally or unintentionally. There are some simple steps to avoid plagiarism, though.

   Keeping good, organized notes as you research is step one. Step two is putting ideas into your own words. Including citations is step three. Remember that evidence and research should supplement, not supplant, your own ideas.

Plagiarism/Not Plagiarism

Source Says

"The good news is, it isn't a bad thing to borrow ideas from other people when delivering a speech. Having sources to back up what you say enhances your credibility and makes for a more engaging speech."

Plagiarism	Not Plagiarism
Speaker Says	*Speaker Says*
I have some good news for you, it is not a bad thing to borrow ideas from other people or things when delivering your speech. In fact, having sources to back your stuff up actually enhances your credibility.	There are many ethical reasons why we should properly attribute sources, but did you know that it can help you as a speaker? In *The Amazing Public Speaking Book*, authors Hannan, Kiger, and Newman argue that source citation can bolster a speaker's credibility.
Why is this plagiarism?	*Why is this not plagiarism?*
Even though the speaker changed or added some details, he is still using the source's ideas without giving the author credit.	The speaker synthesized the information to fit her own needs, then she cited where she found the source idea.

HOW TO CITE SOURCES

Here are some general guidelines for citing your sources. Some speech events may require more information or a different presentation, so check with the organizer.

- **Include enough information so an audience member could locate the source.** On the most basic level, you should include the author, title, and date of publication. In some cases you may not be able to find all this information; some sources (like an essay on a website) may not identify the author or give a publication date. Include whatever information is most relevant to the particular source, best establishes credibility, and will give your audience a sense of where that information comes from.

- **Don't cite websites, cite organizations.** Nearly every news outlet has an online presence, but the source of the information is still the news organization itself. For instance, don't cite "CNN.com," cite "CNN." It is the organization that gives the source credibility, and the web address is unnecessary.

- **Look for the most credible citation possible in each source.** If you are citing a newspaper article, the article will probably include some of its own sources. Johnny Journalist, or whoever wrote the article, most likely is not an expert about whatever the article covers; instead, he probably conducted interviews and did his own research. If he includes a quotation from an actual expert, like Edward Expert, then you can cite Dr. Expert (PhD in Your Topic Area), but then clarify where you found the information as well. For example, "As cited in Johnny Journalist's article, Dr. Expert says mold can sometimes be good." We do advocate, however, that you try to track down Johnny Journalist's sources for yourself; that way, you can cite Dr. Expert directly.

- **Know how to use different moments for your citations.** You can insert your citations into your speech in two places: before the data and in the middle of the data.

  - **Pre-source citations** function as an introduction to the information in the source. For instance:

    The *New York Times* reports that unemployment in the United States has decreased.

    This citation clearly introduces the information and signals to the audience that some research is on its way.

  - **Mid-source citations** occur in the middle of the information being provided from the source. For example:

    Unemployment in the United States, according to the *New York Times*, has decreased.

    This citation begins with the information being cited, then introduces the source, and then concludes the information. This is the most sophisticated form of citation, but it can also be confusing for the audience if not executed clearly.

  - **Avoid post-source citations**, which come after the information being cited has already been delivered. Consider:

    Unemployment in the United States has decreased. That's according to the *New York Times*.

    This sort of citation violates audience expectations. The audience never knows what material is from the speaker's mind or from another source until after the information has been presented.

- **Avoid double citations,** which occur when the speaker introduces the material with the citation language for a single source in two different places. For example:

  According to the April 4th edition of the *New York Times*, it reports that unemployment in the United States has decreased.

  The *New York Times* reports that unemployment in the United States has decreased. It reported this yesterday.

  These examples of double citations are bulky and unclear. Do not do this.

Tying It Together: Authentic Communication

It is humbling to consider how much of the world's collective knowledge is now available at our fingertips, and we might even wonder "What can I add to this?" When confronted with everything everyone has ever said, we must be confident. We must add our own perspective, but when we do, we must make that perspective an informed one.

We can't physically be everywhere or see everything, but good research lets us come pretty close. Research helps us to see through different eyes and to build a more complete picture of our own ideas. Authentic communication is informed communication: inform yourself, and then inform the world.

Doing Super Research (Literally!)

Step 1: Use the research chart below to collect super supporting information about your favorite SUPERHERO or VILLAIN. *Try to use a different source for every question.*

Research Guide	Research	Example
1. Choose a comic book universe:	☐ DC ☐ Marvel	☐ Marvel
2. Choose a side:	☐ Hero ☐ Villain	☐ Hero
3. Find a character in your chosen universe.	_____ [source]	Spider-Man marvel.com
4. In what issue did your character make their comic book debut?	[title of comic] [issue #] [date] [source]	*Amazing Fantasy* Issue #15 (Aug. 1962) techland.time.com
5. What powers does your character have?	_____ _____ [source]	Spider Speed, Spider Grip Spider Sense, Super Smart spiderfan.org

6. What is a weakness of your character? (This may take some digging and thinking.)		emotional sentiment for friends
		underestimating his foes
	[source]	marvel.wikia.com
7. Who is your character's arch enemy?		The Green Goblin
	[source]	comicvine.com
8. What powers does your character's arch enemy have?		superhuman strength
		a regenerative healing factor
	[source]	marveldirectory.com
9. What weaknesses does your character's arch enemy have?		certifiably insane
		obsession with Spider-Man
	[source]	comics.ign.com/ top-100-villains

Step 2: Use your super supporting information to organize a short persuasive speech on why your favorite SUPERHERO or VILLAIN is better than their arch enemy. Try to begin your speech with a strong thesis. Here's an example we developed.

Spider-Man

My favorite superhero of the Marvel Universe is Spider-Man. Because Spider-Man is Super-smart, and because he is not insane, he will always beat his arch enemy, the Green Goblin.

Graeme McMillan of Time magazine revealed that Spider-Man first appeared in Amazing Fantasy Issue

#15 in 1962, and that that issue recently sold for $1.1 million. In the issue, we learn that Spider-Man received his powers by getting a bite from a radioactive spider as a teenager. Spider Fan, a faction of the Comic Boards comic book discussion forum, discusses Spider-Man's powers as being Spider Speed, Spider Grip, and Spider Sense.

But even though his powers are awesome, Marvel Comics Database reveals that he does have weaknesses. He is overly emotional and sentimental about his friends, so he acts irrationally sometimes when they are in danger. He also sometimes underestimates his foes, probably because he is so young.

Comic Vine claims that Spider-Man's arch enemy is the Green Goblin. According to the Marvel Directory, the Green Goblin has superhuman strength and a regenerative healing factor. If Spider-Man wants to beat the Green Goblin, then he must exploit the Goblin's weaknesses. Spider-Man is super smart, so he will check out the Imagine Games Network's Top 100 Villains list to learn that the Goblin's weaknesses are his insanity and his obsession with Spider-Man. Because Spider-Man knows his obsessions, and because he knows that the Goblin will act irrationally, Spider-Man can set a trap for the Green Goblin, but he should make sure his friends are out of harm's way first.

Step 3: Deliver your speech! With all of that hard evidence, we are sure you will be superpersuasive.

Key Concepts

- Research is important for mastering material and building credibility.

- Sources for speeches are all around us.

- Sources should be credible, recent, and appropriate to the tone, setting, and purpose of the speech.

- Use Google and online databases to conduct research utilizing advanced search options.

- When conducting interviews, ask questions that will elicit useful information, and don't forget to say "thank you."

- Cite credible sources in a way that gives the audience enough information to find the source on their own.

- Avoid post-source and double citations.

CHAPTER 7

Organization

In Chapter 1 you learned that every speech has a beginning, a middle, and an end. In more technical language, every speech has an introduction, a body, and a conclusion. Putting the introduction at the beginning and the conclusion at the end isn't complicated, the tricky part is organizing the middle bits. Speeches can be like puzzles; the edge pieces are often the easiest to fit together, but it's the middle that gives us trouble. Chapter 8 will cover introductions and conclusions; this chapter will focus on how to organize the body. First, we will cover how to arrange the big ideas of a speech. Then, we will look at how to keep that structure clear and consistent throughout the speech.

Macro-Organization

After you research your topic and realize that it is much more complicated than you first thought, you have to package the material to further your main speech goal. How you address this task is called "macro-organization," or the order of main ideas in a speech.

The way speeches are organized can be divided into two major categories: undifferentiated and differentiated. In an undifferentiated speech, the speaker has freedom to order his main ideas in any way he chooses; there are no internal demands on the order from the nature of the speech. In a differentiated speech, the organization is determined by its purpose. Let's look at each in more detail.

Category	Defining Characteristic	Example
Undifferentiated Organization	Specific order does not matter; there is no underlying purpose for the speech that would require the main ideas to be presented in a certain way.	*Topic:* "Reasons I Like Roller Coasters" The speaker could have a variety of reasons to like roller coasters and could present them in any order. The audience doesn't need to hear one idea in order to understand the next idea.
Differentiated Organization	Order matters; the speech would not make sense unless it is organized in a particular way.	*Topic:* "How To Assemble a Bicycle" The speaker couldn't start with the last step of the assembly process as the first idea in his speech; he'd end up with a funky-looking bicycle.

UNDIFFERENTIATED SPEECH ORGANIZATION

As we've seen, in an undifferentiated speech the speaker can arrange his main ideas as he chooses. Still, a speaker should make purposeful choices when organizing his speech, and several structures will work in a variety of situations.

- **Main ideas can be organized chronologically.** Humans have a natural ability to organize ideas chronologically; so, if there is any natural flow of time between ideas, chronological organization can work well. The ideas are presented in time order; the history of a subject might come first, and then each subsequent point moves through the past to the present and future. For instance, a speech about computers could have the following main ideas:

  1. The invention of computers

  2. The first personal computer

  3. Modern computing technology

  4. The future of computing technology

  Here's another example, this time about golf:

  1. Getting the right equipment

  2. Perfecting your swing

  3. The rules of the course

  It's a little less obvious, but this outline is also chronological: to play golf, you need to first obtain the right equipment, then practice your swing, then go to a course and play a round. Even if a topic doesn't have an obvious history-present-future organization, you can still present it in a chronological way that will enhance your audience's understanding.

- **Main ideas can be organized spatially.** Another way that people naturally organize ideas is spatial; that is, they visualize the ideas laid out in some pattern or as moving from one location to another. Spatial organization can take a variety of forms: geographic organization, internal to external organization, or even just moving around a room. Let's look at some examples. First, an informative speech about the cello might be organized thus:

  1. The Base of the Cello: Proper Posture

  2. The Heart of the Cello: Producing Good Tone

  3. The Top of the Cello: Tuning and Tune

  This speech moves from the bottom of the cello to the top, creating a strong image that helps the audience understand the organization of the speech.

  Here's another example from a speech about rap:

  1. New York: The Origin of Rap

  2. The West Coast: Gangster Rap and the Hyphy Movement

  3. The Dirty South: Trill, Trap, and Chop

  This speech breaks up the various forms and styles of rap into geographical areas, and, again, reinforces the structure for the audience through the use of an image.

- **Main ideas can be organized by value or moral worth.** You can also organize your ideas using categories like the pros and cons of a subject. This structure allows the speaker to paint a balanced picture of his topic and works especially well if the speaker doesn't have a strong opinion about the issue. Here is an example from a speech about pumas.

1. The Pros of Pumas

   A. Can be very handsome

   B. Can jump over 40 feet

   C. Have beautiful fur

2. The Cons of Pumas

   A. Can kill you

   B. Do not make good pets

   C. Can smell bad

Here, the audience gets a complete picture of the puma, the handsome menace of the American southwest. Moving from "good" to "bad" or from "bad" to "good" helps the audience feel like they have seen both sides of an issue, and so will have a more positive impression of the speaker.

- **Main ideas can be organized from small to large or the inconsequential to the important.** This organization could rely on physical characteristics (like talking about mice and then elephants), but we mean it more figuratively. If you've got information that you need to present for context but is unimportant for establishing your major point, put it first in your speech. That way, you can "get it out of the way" before moving onto the important issues. By telling the audience that this is what you are doing, you reassure them and encourage them to pay more attention as the speech goes on. (The audience would otherwise, just by virtue of being an audience, slowly lose interest as time progresses.) Let's look at an example of this organization using the topic Zoos: Good, Clean Fun? Or Prison for Animals?

1. Distinguishing Between Zoos and Wildlife Preserves

2. Zoos Don't Offer Ideal Habitats

3. Many Zoo Animals Display Abnormal Behavior

This sample outline begins with an explanation of what constitutes a zoo; this section of the speech is largely definitional, and doesn't get at the core idea of the speech. The second and third parts of the speech, though, make direct, compelling arguments in support of the thesis, and are more likely to be interesting to the audience.

Note: It's okay to reverse the order of physical things (talk about elephants and then mice), but not of ideas. It's never a good idea to end with inconsequential details; the audience will just be angry that you kept them around for that extra two minutes to discuss something that doesn't matter. Deal with the little things first; save the big ideas for last.

- **Main ideas can be organized any way you can imagine, as long as you explain the organizing principle to the audience.** Want to present your ideas alphabetically? Great. Tell your audience that's what you're doing. Want to talk about progressively more expensive things you can spend your lotto winnings on? Good idea. Tell your audience that's what you're doing.

Always provide reasoning for whatever structure you've chosen. Doing so will help the audience anticipate, follow, and remember your speech by presenting the ideas in a way that makes sense to the human brain. The only unacceptable choice when speaking is to just throw ideas out randomly and hope the audience makes sense of them.

DIFFERENTIATED SPEECH ORGANIZATION

Some speeches have specific structures and purposes that require each paragraph to accomplish a particular task. These tasks are determined by the purpose of the speech as a whole, and can vary widely. We will focus on the two most common types of speeches, informative and persuasive speeches, to illustrate some differentiated structures.

Informative Speaking

In an informative speech, the speaker takes on the role of the teacher, explaining a concept or phenomenon. The goal is for the audience to walk away from the speech with a solid understanding of the speaker's subject matter. The undifferentiated chronological order works well for informative speeches, particularly if you are informing your audience about a specific historical figure or event. Spatial organization can also work well if you are informing your audience how to play the guitar or explaining Mongolian expansion. However, the speaker may also choose any of the following structures:

- **Description/Application/Implications.** This is the most straightforward option for an informative speech. The speaker begins by describing the subject of the speech, defining it for the audience; then she explains how the subject is applied or used in the world, helping the audience to put the topic in context. Finally, she explains the implications of the speech, helping the audience to understand its importance and relevance to their lives. Here is a sample outline using the topic Understanding Genetically Modified Organisms (GMOs).

  1. The definition and development of GMOs

  2. Global GMO usage

3. How do GMOs affect you?

The speech begins by providing a working definition of and some background information about genetically modified organisms, then demonstrates how GMOs are used, and ends by discussing how they affect the audience directly. Definition and application are important, but speakers often focus on them to the exclusion of implication. The speaker must always relate the subject of the speech to the audience. This important step helps the audience appreciate the subject, and thus makes them more likely to remember the speech.

- **Description/Benefits and Drawbacks/Implications.** This is a slight variation on Description/Application/Implications structure that allows the speaker to more fully engage with controversial subject matter. This structure includes definition and implication but looks at the benefits and disadvantages of the subject rather than just its applications. Let's apply this structure to the subject of genetically modified organisms.

1. The definition and development of GMOs

2. Benefits and drawbacks of GMOs

    A. GMOs help combat famine

    B. GMOs may cause the extinction of native species

3. How do GMOs affect you?

This speech acknowledges the sometimes-contentious debate over GMOs by explaining their pros and cons. The third section will probably reflect some sort of resolution to this tension, but it does not need to. This structure brings the informative speaker closer to making an argument but also allows him to remain as neutral as he likes.

Persuasive Speaking

In a persuasive speech, the speaker takes on the role of the advocate. The goal of this type of speech is to convince the audience to enact some change to the status quo (the current state of things). The following are some of the structures available to those who seek to persuade.

- **Problem/Solution.** If you want the audience to change something, you need to convince them that it needs changing. This is where a basic "Problem/Solution" structure can be useful. Begin by outlining the problem in the status quo, then lay out the solutions to that problem. Here is a sample outline:

1. The Problem with Zoos

    A. Zoos don't offer ideal habitats

    B. Many zoo animals display abnormal behavior

2. Fixing Our Zoo Problems

    A. Habitats need to be more expansive and enriching

    B. Animals need companionship and compassionate care

If you use this structure, be sure your solutions actually address the problems you highlight. If your solutions to the problems identified above were to charge less for zoo admission and give every visitor cotton candy, then you would have failed at your task.

- **Problem/Cause/Solution.** Another option for organizing persuasive speeches is to include an analysis of what causes the problem. This can help the speaker craft (and the audience understand) the proposed solutions. This approach is also more nuanced than a problem/solution format. Consider our zoo example again. If we move to a problem/cause/solution format, we might reorganize the material like this:

  1. *The Problem:* Zoos cause many animals to become depressed

  2. *The Cause:* Zoo habitats are often less than ideal

  3. *The Solution:* Zoo habitats need to be larger and more varied

  By identifying the cause of the problem, the poor habitat quality, we can focus in on a specific solution to the problem.

- **Cause/Effect/Solution.** We can emphasize causes even more by using this structure. This structure covers similar content as the problem/cause/solution, but it puts causes first and problems second. Here is an example, about the legalization of marijuana:

  1. The prohibition of marijuana forces users into the black market (cause)

  2. The black market contributes to the power and reach of drug cartels (effect)

  3. Legalizing marijuana eliminates the black market and associated violence (solution)

This approach enables the speaker to establish a tighter link between causes and effects, which can also lead to clearer solutions.

- **Comparative Advantages.** If you are speaking about a problem that has two or more viable, though distinct solutions, you might utilize a comparative advantages speech structure. In this structure, the speaker outlines the potential solutions to the problem and then discusses the advantages and disadvantages of each. Eventually, through the process of elimination, the most viable solution emerges.

  Imagine discussing your Saturday night plans with friends. You carefully weigh each proposal, but you know what solution you want the audience (your friends) to adopt; so at each moment you compare solutions. It's important to keep in mind that the comparative advantages structure should be used only if everyone already agrees that there is a problem that needs solving.

- **Monroe's Motivated Sequence.** Alan Monroe, who was a professor of communication at Purdue University, believed that when we encounter a problem we naturally look for solutions. Consequently, our role as persuaders is to direct the audience's attention to the problem and they'll want to know what they can do to fix it. Monroe designed a series of steps, known as Monroe's Motivated Sequence[1], for persuasive speeches to inspire the audience to take action.

  Step 1: Attention. Gain the attention of the audience. To draw attention to your issue, ask yourself what drew you to this topic in the first place. How will you generate that same level of interest in your audience? You want to show your audience that this subject is one they should listen to and care about.

Step 2: Need. Explain why the problem is relevant to the audience.

Step 3: Satisfaction. Explain the specific solution to the problem and demonstrate how the proposed solution will address the problem.

Step 4: Visualization. Detail how the world will look if the audience does or does not accept the solution proposed.

Step 5: Action. Tell the audience exactly what they can do to contribute to solving the problem.

HANDLING WEAK POINTS

Possibly the most common question we field when discussing organization is "Where do I put my weakest point?" Speakers are always nervous about the relative strengths of their ideas and concerned about how to best "'hide" their weakest idea. So what do you do? First, you can organize your points using one of the structures above. Don't order the points of your speech by strength or affinity; develop a structure that makes sense and helps the audience process your ideas collectively.

Assuming you've got some options for organization, don't put your weakest point first or last. If you put it first, you run the risk of losing the audience; if the speech is weak to start, the audience may give up hope of a stronger middle or end. If you put it last, you can ruin a great speech with a deflated ending.

So put weakest points in the middle of a speech. If you've got three ideas, then it's best if the weakest idea is second. This organization preserves a strong beginning that captures the audience's attention and a compelling conclusion that will likely be remembered. It's not ideal (you shouldn't have weak points), but sometimes it's the best you can do.

Micro-Organization

No matter how clear your overall structure, no matter how tightly the pieces fit together and how well you've organized your ideas, you still need to help the audience follow along. After you've made your macro-organizational choices and arranged your ideas, it's time to actually connect them. To do this you use previews, reviews, and transitions.

PREVIEWS

The first tool you can use to keep your audience informed is a preview. Previews are typically located in the introduction of a speech; they follow the thesis and lay out the structure of the speech for the audience. Previews are sometimes called *roadmaps* because they let the audience know where they will be going (on a speech adventure!).

You can also use a preview in the body of the speech to give the audience extra structural support. This is sometimes called an *internal preview*, because it introduces what you will talk about in the point. If a speaker is going to list some things, like different ways to cook carrots, a preview could be useful in helping the audience keep the structure clear. Let's consider some examples:

> Because *The Invisible Man* makes such a powerful argument about race and identity, it should not be banned by any school district in the United States. To better understand why, we will first examine the story, then look at its impact on

American literature, and finally explore the role that race plays in American education.

There are three different ways to cook carrots: boil them, steam them, or microwave them.

The first example would work as a preview in an introduction; the speaker would then transition into his first main idea, which is the story of *The Invisible Man*. The second example would work as an internal preview within a main idea—cooking carrots. To better understand this example, let's look at an outline for this speech about the life cycle of carrots.

1. How carrots are farmed

2. How carrots are prepared for the supermarket

3. How carrots are cooked

    A. Boiling carrots

    B. Steaming carrots

    C. Microwaving carrots

Following the internal preview of point 3, the speaker would expand on each method of cooking carrots.

REVIEWS

Typically, reviews are the first element a speaker might include in her conclusion. Reviews tell the audience what she just told them; they work like scrapbooks. A review looks back at the main ideas covered in the speech and gives the audience an opportunity to collect their thoughts. You can also use a review at the end of a main idea or section of a speech if that section was particularly dense. This is sometimes called an *internal summary*. Here are some examples of reviews:

> Today, we learned about the book *The Invisible Man*, how it affected American literature, and the role race plays in American education.

> So, to review, the carrots are first planted in rows, then fertilized, and then harvested by hand ten to twelve weeks later.

The first example would serve as an excellent review at the end of our speech. The second example could function as an internal summary or a review at the end of a single point about the farming process for carrots.

Previews and reviews are helpful for the audience and for the speaker. The audience benefits from the additional exposition and opportunity to think about the speech or idea as a whole. A speaker benefits from previews and reviews because they give her an opportunity to reinforce her memorization process (with extra repetition) and check for comprehension from the audience (with an extra opportunity to look for nodding heads).

TRANSITIONS

We use transitions to move from idea to idea. If previews are roadmaps, then transitions are signposts: they give the audience information about the speech as you move along. Strong transitions have four components:

1. **Strong transitions use transition words that develop the relationships between ideas.** Transition words express a relationship between ideas; they connect words, sentences, or paragraphs. For example:

Use	Possible transition words
To continue or build on an idea:	Additionally
	Also
	And
	As well as
	As a matter of fact
	Furthermore
	Not only . . . but also . . .
	Moreover
To clarify a complex concept:	In other words
	Basically
	That is to say
	To put it another way
	What I mean is
To introduce an illustration or example of an idea:	For example
	For instance
	For one thing
	Like
	Most notably
	To illustrate this
To show conflict between ideas:	But
	However
	In contrast
	Conversely
	On the other hand
	When in fact
	Although

To emphasize an idea:	Above all
	Even more
	Indeed
	Most importantly
To show a cause and effect relationship:	So
	As a result of this
	Consequently
	Because of this
	Given that
	Hence
	Thus
	Therefore

2. **Strong transitions reinforce the language of the speech.**
   Transitions reinforce the relationships between ideas by using the language of the ideas themselves. A speaker can do this by repeating her main objective and coupling it with the information that is to follow. Consider a speech by a representative for Americans for a Healthy Diet. The thesis of the speech might be "You should avoid trans fats." In order to use strong transitions, the representative will refer to this specific language throughout the speech:

   > The next reason to avoid trans fats is because they lower life expectancy.

   This transition uses a transition word (*next*) and also uses the language of the thesis.

3. **Strong transitions reinforce the different levels of analysis in an outline.** They help the audience follow along as the speaker moves from big-picture ideas to particular details and back again.

A good outline has many levels of analysis. There are the main ideas of the speech. Then the main ideas often have sub-topics or explanations, and these sub-topics and explanations might have sub-sub-topics and sub-explanations. Let's look at our sample outline about the life cycle of carrots.

Thesis: The Three Phases of the Life Cycle of Carrots

1. How carrots are farmed

2. How carrots are prepared for the supermarket

3. How carrots are cooked

   A. Boiling carrots

   B. Steaming carrots

   C. Microwaving carrots

This outline has three main ideas: farming carrots, preparing carrots for sale, and cooking carrots. The third main idea has three smaller ideas included in it: boiling, steaming, microwaving. The transitional language that the speaker uses between main idea 1 and main idea 2 should be different from the transitional language he uses between smaller ideas 3-A and 3-B. Consider:

> The second main phase of a carrot's life cycle is the trip to the supermarket.

This example uses big-picture language (it references the thesis and uses the word *main*).

> A second way to cook carrots is by steaming them.

This example uses the more focused language of main idea 3 (cook carrots by steaming them). It also maintains a separate ordering system for the sub-points. Using full transitions like this will help your audience understand and process your carrot speech.

4. **Strong transitions use retrospective and prospective language.** Retrospective language is language that reviews information that has already been covered. Prospective language describes what is coming up.

Let's imagine a speaker is giving a presentation on the invention of laptop computing and its impact on the economy. The speaker's first point of analysis may be the history of the laptop and the second point of analysis may be a description of contemporary office culture. In order to transition between these points, the speaker may say, "Now that we've learned about the history of the laptop, let's explore contemporary office culture." This transition connects the past point with the next point, which makes it an excellent transition.

▓ SPEAKER SPOTLIGHT

Mario Nguyen
Student, Harvard Law

Mario Nguyen began competing in speech and debate in the 3rd grade. Since then he has been awarded a Fulbright grant to Mexico, a Princeton-in-Asia Fellowship, and is currently pursuing a degree at Harvard Law School. Mario is a first-generation American and the first person in his family to graduate high school. As a law student, Mario understands that organizing his ideas is paramount before delivering them to an audience.

I gave a speech at the National Equality March in D.C. The venue rallied 200,000 people and several media outlets. It was incredible because I got to advocate and be a voice for something I cared so deeply about: human rights.

No matter what capacity you work in, you have to communicate—whether it be with your boss, coworkers, or customers.

Speech is the ultimate life preparation that spreads across all careers.

I excelled in school because of public speaking; I already knew how to organize my thoughts and back them with research.

I have seen socially awkward kids leave speech [as a competitive activity] completely different and with more self-confidence than ever before.

Relax. Be conversational and talk to the audience as if you were talking to your best friend.

Don't lose your original style. People will try to make you look like everyone else. That's gross. Be you and own it.

VEHICLES

Transitional vehicles are recurring devices that add consistency and interest to transitions. They are called vehicles because they help the speaker (and the audience) get from point A to point B. Here are some examples of vehicles in preview statements. (The vehicles are in italics):

> To better understand the profession of paramedics, let's *ride along* with them on a typical call. First, we'll *take down* some background information; then we'll apply some *first aid* in the form of modern practices; and finally we'll *release our patient* with some information to take home about education and employment statistics"

Let's follow along with the life cycle of a carrot. It starts out as a *seed* at the farm; then it will be *harvested* and shipped to the supermarket; and then *ends up on the dinner table*. It's a long journey, but we'll learn along the way.

These preview statements not only lay out the content of the speech, but also provide the audience with a unique way to understand its structure. At each major transition, the speaker will use these vehicles to keep the audience engaged.

To be fair, not every vehicle needs to be so metaphorical; a vehicle can be a powerful story threaded throughout the speech. For example, a student once delivered a persuasive speech about the dangers associated with the unregulated in-home daycare industry. As she transitioned from point to point, she would tell a new (often horrifying) story of the conditions in some daycare centers. Each story served as a compelling vehicle, carrying the speaker from one point to the next. Be they funny, somber, or compelling, vehicles are a great way to add coherency and polish to any speech.

Tying It Together: Authentic Communication

Organization is essential for a successful speech. If you are organized, if the structure of your speech is coherent and clearly explained, then the audience will be more able and more willing to follow along. More to the point, you will be better able to express your ideas clearly and confidently.

Authentic communication requires clarity of thought, and working hard to organize your personal perspective produces that clarity. Everyone has something to say, and everyone has the potential to say it wonderfully. Organization unlocks that potential: it gives us a roadmap to self-expression.

Organization

You are in a real pickle. Someone vandalized the local playground with red spray paint. Worse than that, a graffiti message says that "(insert your name) did this!" and the local authorities found six empty cans of red spray paint on the ground just outside of your garage door.

Your mission: Use the materials below to construct a speech that will PERSUADE the local authorities that you had nothing to do with this heinous crime.

Step 1: Brainstorm.

Use the table below to help you generate your airtight alibi. Use the left column for an undifferentiated approach, with three unrelated arguments. Use the right for a differentiated approach, with a comparative advantages model.

Undifferentiated	Differentiated
Reasons you could not have done this (example: This is a fictitious premise. I don't even have a garage, leave me alone.)	Using a comparative advantages model, argue for your release (example: If I am punished, I will be upset. If I am released, I will praise the city's justice.)
Alibi 1: (physical impossibility)	A. Poor Solution 1: Punish me
Alibi 2: (explain the spray paint)	B. Poor Solution 2: Shut down the playground.
Alibi 3: (no motive)	C. Ideal Solution: Let me go, and proclaim my innocence.

Step 2: Construct and Speak.
Add transitions between the paragraphs and deliver the speech with ethos, logos, and pathos! Convince those local authorities that you love children and you love playgrounds.

Key Concepts

- Every speech has two levels of organization: macro-organization, which is the arrangement of main ideas in the speech, and micro-organization, which is the way ideas are joined together.

- Macro-organization can take two forms: undifferentiated, where the order of ideas doesn't matter, and differentiated, where the purpose of the speech requires a specific order of ideas.

- Undifferentiated ideas can be arranged in a variety of ways—for example, spatially, chronologically, or by size—as long as the organization makes sense to you and you explain it to your audience.

- Differentiated speeches include many possible structures for both informative and persuasive speeches.

- Previews and reviews help organize complicated ideas and help the audience anticipate and/or process the information presented.

- Transitions help connect ideas and arguments.

- Vehicles can add interest and coherency to transitions.

CHAPTER 8

Introductions and Conclusions

The introduction to a speech sets the tone for the entire presentation. If the introduction is underdeveloped, then the audience may think that the speech is not very important and will not give it their full attention. If the introduction is bloated with extra-analysis, then the audience may be confused about the organization of the speech and will not grasp the intended focus. Additionally, the audience will use the introduction to judge whether or not you are a credible presenter.

And even a perfectly crafted speech, with a fantastic introduction, can be ruined by a mediocre conclusion. The conclusion is the last thing the audience will hear, and the thing they will be most likely to remember. It will cement their memory of your speech as either good or bad.

That is a whole lot of pressure jammed into two components of your speech, and that is exactly why you must build your introductions and conclusions with care. But don't fret, in this chapter, we are going to show you how to use introductions and conclusions as an opportunity to really impress your audience.

Introduction to Introductions

Every strong introduction must accomplish several objectives, and these objectives can be organized into distinct sections:

Attention-getting Device (AGD)

Link

Justification

Thesis

Preview

Notice the order; it is always the same.

Attention-getting Devices, or First Impressions Are Last Chances

The first objective of an introduction is to capture the audience's attention. It is incredibly important that your first few words, ideas, and sentences be interesting. If they are not, you are likely to lose your audience right away. Remember, the audience doesn't know you yet and they haven't heard any good reason to keep listening. If you start strong, though, you will build credibility and the audience will be more likely to forgive future mistakes.

In order to capture the audience's attention, every speech should begin with an Attention-getting Device. The AGD is also sometimes called "the hook" in writing classes. A good AGD has a few characteristics.

- **A good AGD is interesting.** "Interesting" is an overused word, but we literally mean that the speaker should want the audience to be interested in what happens next. When the speaker begins her presentation, the worst outcome is for the audience to lose interest because they either know or don't care what is coming. You want the audience to be asking questions like "Where is this going?" or "What is this speech going to be about?," not wondering "How much longer do we have to be here?" or "Maybe we should leave early to beat traffic." You want to generate interest.

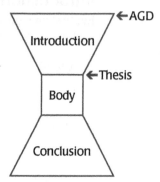

We will explore some different approaches to constructing an AGD in the next section, but for now we will focus on some general applications. An introduction that jumps right into the content of a speech causes the audience to drift away because they are not prepared for your message. They need to be enticed into listening. The AGD is that enticement! The audience will also lose concentration if you open with a cacophony of clichéd language. Nothing says, "PLEASE DON'T LISTEN TO ME," more than an introduction full of old adages, familiar sayings, and unoriginal ideas. Clichéd language screams, "I didn't work very hard on this speech," so the audience will respond accordingly—by turning their attention to something else.

If the speaker sounds like someone the audience has heard before, then why would they listen? So, always aim for a unique or vivid idea in the AGD.

Consider these examples:

> Hello. I am here today to talk about the internal combustion engine.

> A wise man once said, "Every journey begins with a single step."

> Right now, millions of precisely controlled explosions are propelling thousands of people to and from work.

The first example is boring and unimaginative; the second relies on an overused, generic quotation that the audience has heard many times; the third presents an unusual and exciting perspective on the topic. As a bonus, it is has a little intrigue; the audience will naturally wonder what comes next. Now that the audience is interested, the speaker can lead them willingly to his topic.

- **A good AGD starts with a broad focus, then works its way toward a specific topic.** Many beginning writers or speakers jump right into their topic or even begin with their thesis statement. This is a mistake. The audience isn't familiar with the speaker yet, and they may not even be willing to listen to anything serious. A good AGD begins with something interesting that isn't specifically about the speaker's focus.

To help visualize this, picture the introduction as an hourglass. The introduction begins broadly, and then focuses down toward the thesis sentence. The AGD is the first element in the introduction, and so it will be the broadest of the concepts and the furthest from the focus of the speech. Consider this simple example:

The world is a big place. It has many different nations, all of which are unique and interesting. Nigeria is one of those nations. Nigeria is unique among nations because of its natural beauty, friendly population, and compelling history.

This really simple example demonstrates how an introduction should work: it begins broadly and works its way to a narrowly focused thesis. The opening idea, "The world is a big place," doesn't give away too much at once; it keeps the audience guessing what will come next, and so generates interest.

- **A good AGD sets the tone for the speech.** Attention-getting Devices must match the tone of the speech. If you are about to deliver a persuasive speech about an issue that affects people's lives, cracking jokes during the introduction isn't advisable. AGDs should be interesting, and maybe even a little odd, but never so absurd or disrespectful that they compromise the speaker's integrity.

- **A good AGD reinforces the ideas of the speech.** Some speakers opt for AGDs that get attention just for attention's sake. For example,

  THE BUILDING IS ON FIRE, EVERYBODY RUN TO THE EXIT! Just kidding, but now that I have your attention, let's talk about greenhouse gases.

This AGD grabs the audience's attention but the attention is not meaningful; it violates the audience's expectations. Good AGDs generate interest *in the topic area to be discussed.* Speakers can use ideas that will be explored later in the speech, a fresh perspective on the topic as a whole, or an illustration to capture the audience's attention and build momentum.

Getting the Audience's Attention!

You can construct an AGD in many ways. You can:

- **Use facts and figures.** You can begin with an interesting fact or figure that is designed to impress or intrigue the audience. Many people refer to this type of introduction as a "statistics" introduction, but that can be misleading. "Statistics" suggests some dry or complicated number, but this kind of introduction can actually be quite simple and straightforward. For example:

  There are more than 2,000 species of jellyfish in the ocean. There's cannonball jelly, mushroom jelly, Lion's Mane jelly, and others. Let's learn about them.

  A stealth bomber costs nearly one billion dollars to manufacture. This remarkably sophisticated piece of machinery is fine-tuned every day by a team of mechanics, engineers, and support staff, and they have no margin for error. Maintaining cutting-edge aircraft is just one example of the exciting careers available in the United States Air Force.

  The first example uses an interesting number, but then does nothing to expand on it. It just lies there, like a jellyfish washed up on the beach. The second example, though, effectively paints a vivid picture in the audience's mind with an impressive fact about stealth bombers.

Both examples use facts that relate directly to their topic, which makes linking the AGD to the topic easier. The first example relates a little *too* directly, however. It doesn't start broad enough, and so the audience has no time to process or wonder what the speech will be about; the statistic used as the AGD might make more sense in the body of that particular speech. The second example, by contrast, does a good job using a fact that is slightly off-topic, then works its way to the actual focus of the speech.

- **Use hypothetical situations or imaginary stories.** Some topics are best illustrated by a story, either hypothetical or real. Consider this example.

  > Imagine you are driving down a country road late at night. There are no streetlamps, and your headlights reveal only a portion of the road ahead. Suddenly, a deer crosses the road; you try to avoid it, but it's too late. This scenario could be avoided if your car was equipped with radar; this might sound like science fiction, but soon, radar will be a standard feature on all cars.

  This AGD effectively illustrates a main idea of the speech— the potential of radar-equipped cars. It also generates tension and excites the interest of the audience.

- **Use real anecdotes.** An anecdote is a short story; it can be historical or contemporary, general or specific, funny or serious. Theoretically, anecdotes can be fictional; for our purposes, though, we encourage you to use true stories. Not only are they typically more interesting (because they have real, accurate details), but they also communicate to the audience that you did some research. When you start with "Imagine a boy in the middle of the ocean...," the audience may just hear "I couldn't find an example of this actually happening, but please don't leave just yet." Here are two examples of anecdotes used as AGDs:

> In the 17th century, a man named Thomas realized his family was out of food. So he went down to the local castle and asked for work. He wasn't given any work, and instead his family was thrown into prison for being poor. This sort of story was all too common, and something had to change. That change was democracy.

> During the Cuban Missile Crisis, Pres. John F. Kennedy needed to reach the Secretary of State; he called, but nobody answered the phone. The President realized what a threat this posed to the country, and so he ordered that a State Department staffer be provided with a telephone, a desk, and a cot, so the phone could be answered 24 hours a day. Thus was born the State Department Watch Room, a round-the-clock communications hub for American diplomacy.

The first example is plainly fictional, and is also very vague. Where was this? Who was Thomas? How did this particular story relate to the topic, democracy? This AGD misses an opportunity to impart some important, compelling content on the audience. The second example, though, is true, fascinating, and instructive. True, compelling anecdotes tell stories, contain conflict, and clearly relate to the topic to be discussed. If you are struggling to find an AGD, take a lesson from President Kennedy: do what needs to be done, and find an interesting true story to tell about your topic.

- **Use fables or allegories.** A fable is a short story that features animals or inanimate objects that have been given human qualities (like talking teapots or nostalgic foxes). An allegory is a story (a short one, for an AGD) with a hidden meaning (for example, a pair of siblings fighting might represent the relationship between Europe and the United States). Typically, these types of stories are imaginative and fun; they require that the speaker understands her subject well enough to create a relevant story and is inventive enough to make it entertaining.

You can use existing stories to craft fables and allegories, perhaps by changing human characters into animals or inanimate objects; you can even use existing fables and allegories (like the Tortoise and the Hare, or Pilgrim's Progress). Creating your own stories, though, allows you to be more on-topic. Here are two examples:

> A stapler and a sheet of paper were discussing the American economy. The sheet of paper thought the economy was fine, but the stapler thought it could do better if America cooperated with China. The stapler was right.

> A man begins a journey with a pebble in his shoe. He ignores it. Soon, he is chased by a flock of angry birds; then he is attacked by a pack of wild dogs; finally, he falls into a tiger pit. At the bottom of the pit, he bends down and removes the pebble from his shoe. The man is the United States Congress, and the pebble is the reforming of the Electoral College. Congress has bigger things to worry about.[1]

The first example simply uses inanimate objects to have a boring conversation about the topic of the speech; it teaches nothing. The second example, though, is unique and fresh; the audience has not heard it before because it is new and specifically designed for the topic. It tells a story that is clear and straightforward, so the audience is able to follow along, and it links clearly and robustly to the topic.

- **Use quotations.** Quotations are the most common way to begin a speech and probably have been for a very long time. This long history speaks to the tried-and-true nature of quotation AGDs, and also to how overused they are. As we'll discuss later, quotations work well as conclusions, but we advise you to try other AGD techniques first. If you must use a quotation to begin your speech, you can do several things to make it seem fresh. First, don't select a quotation you've heard before; your audience has probably heard it too, and you won't be gaining any points for originality. Second, be sure to select a quotation that speaks directly to your topic and not to a vague principle. Finally, try to add your own analysis or wit to the AGD; you don't want your audience to remember someone else's words more than your own. Here is an example of a well-executed quotation AGD:

> Adlai Stevenson, an American politician and diplomat once said that "Peace is the one condition of survival in this nuclear age." As we face new threats emerging from every corner of the globe, we must always keep these words in mind and work not just to obtain a secure future, but to secure a peaceful future.

This introduction begins with an uncommon quotation, has a clear link between the quotation and the topic, and includes some additional language that adds to the impact of the quotation. If you're using a quotation, you could do a lot worse than this. That said, if you don't use a quotation, you could probably do a lot better than this, too.

Include a Link

After presenting an Attention-getting Device, a speaker must link the AGD to her topic. The link is the speaker's opportunity to introduce her topic to the audience: she must capitalize on the momentum of her AGD and redirect the audience's attention to whatever it is she wants to talk about. The link is also sometimes called the *pivot* because it is the moment the speaker turns from her AGD to her topic. A strong link has two characteristics.

1. **A strong link is sophisticated.** It doesn't beat the audience over the head with the connection between ideas. Rather, it subtly transitions from the AGD to the topic.

   One common form of link is a *simile*, or a comparison that uses "like" or "as." For example:

   > In Mark Twain's book, *The Adventures of Huck-leberry Finn*, the main character learns many lessons about race and racism. The United States is like Huck Finn, in that we are still learning many lessons about race.

   The link is not very clear, and so this AGD feels forced. Often, speakers resort to similes to indicate the link because the link is not strong and needs to be spelled out. If the link were stronger, then the speaker would not need to say that the AGD is "like" the topic; it would already be apparent to the audience.

   Stronger links are clearer to the audience, and can often be communicated through *metaphor*, or a comparison that simply equates two unlike things. Let's revisit the AGD about the man with a pebble in his shoe:

A man begins a journey with a pebble in his shoe. He ignores it. Soon, he is chased by a flock of angry birds; then he is attacked by a pack of wild dogs; finally, he falls into a tiger pit. At the bottom of the pit, he bends down and removes the pebble from his shoe. The man is the United States Congress, and the pebble is the reforming of the Electoral College; the Congress has bigger things to worry about.

This metaphor works because the AGD is on topic and so the link is already solidly constructed.

2. **A strong link balances out the AGD.** It does this in two ways. First, a strong link is contextually matched to the length of the AGD. If the AGD is short—between two and four sentences—the link can be relatively short as well, between two and three sentences. As the AGD grows longer, the link should keep pace. The audience needs to be gradually brought around to the focus of the topic.

The second way a strong link balances out the AGD is by disarming the audience. A strong AGD is often unusual or unexpected and so the audience struggles to keep up. This sort of confusion can be a powerful tool at the outset of a speech. If a guy walks into a store shouting something in a foreign language, people will be confused but will want to figure out what's going on; but if, after people are paying attention, he explains what he needs, his audience will better understand him (because of the attention they were paying).

Justification

The third component of a strong introduction is the *justification*, or the speaker's explanation for why the topic is worth the audience's attention. Consider this AGD:

> A young woman steps out of a helicopter atop a building; she is carrying a small cooler. Inside is a human heart. She is rushing to provide the organ for a transplant patient. This scene is becoming increasingly common today, and it's about time. Thousands of Americans are awaiting an organ transplant, and thanks to new technologies and techniques, they may finally receive one.

The speaker explains that because scientists have made tremendous strides in regenerative medicine, and because thousands of people are awaiting an organ transplant, the audience should listen closely to the speech. What's that you say, Mr. Speaker? Listening to this speech will save lives? I can't wait to listen! And that's exactly how you want your audience to feel.

The Thesis

The thesis of a speech packages the speaker's message in a clear, concise, and compelling way. Typically, the thesis will be near the end of your introduction. As discussed in Chapter 5, the thesis should declare the purpose of your speech, or what you aim to accomplish through your public address.

You also learned that to create a great thesis, you should justify your purpose or claim with a "because" statement, for example, "Because we all love swimming, we should all move near the ocean," could be the thesis of your speech about embracing Global Warming as a good thing. Your "because" statement would continue the logic that you established in your link and justification sections. Let's explore some examples in the following exercise.

Time to Play: Good Thesis/Bad Thesis!

Read the Theses
Choose which is the Good Thesis and which is the Bad Thesis.

A	B
1. I like marshmallows.	Because they are so vital to the making of Rice Krispie® treats, S'mores, and Granny's sweet potato casserole, the marshmallow is a vital part of any family vacation.
2. Because we own the beat, and because the beat gives life to the streets, then we also own these streets.	We own the beat and these streets.
3. Because too much bad cholesterol can lead to heart disease, people should avoid using butter in excess when cooking.	Butter is bad for you.

Solution: 1b, 2a, 3a

Notice how the message is more specific in the better theses (the answers are upside down at the bottom). Specificity is important for your thesis. Your thesis should communicate exactly what you want to say. The thesis isn't the time to hint or suggest. Say exactly what you mean.

Your thesis should end with a *preview* that communicates the organization of the speech to the audience. The preview acts like a roadmap, and once the audience hears it, they know what to expect. Here is a possible preview after one of the theses from above (preview in italics):

> Because too much bad cholesterol can lead to heart disease, people should avoid using butter in excess when cooking. In order to better understand the benefit of not using butter, *we will look at the biological effects butter has on our bodies. Then we will explore some safe alternatives to keep the flavor without putting your heart at risk.*

The purpose of the speech is communicated clearly in the thesis: people should avoid using butter in excess when cooking. Then the next two sentences preview how the speech will be organized to prove the thesis. The first part of the speech will address the effect butter has on our bodies. The second part will offer alternatives to cooking with butter. If the speaker tells the audience where he is going, the audience will be more likely to pay attention.

SPEAKER SPOTLIGHT

Nadine Ajaka
Freelance Journalist

Nadine spent two years serving humanitarian aid organizations in Jordan and Iraq while also working as a freelance journalist for Al Jazeera English. She is now beginning a new chapter in Washington DC in the video department of The Atlantic magazine. As a journalist, Nadine knows that without a solid introduction, you lose your audience.

I spent four years on Ohio University's speech and debate team. For me, it was one of the most formative experiences I could have had as a person.

I work mostly with Syrian refugees and the displaced, gathering their stories and uncovering bits about their lives to share in a way that preserves their dignity as people. I have to be sensitive because the political landscape in the Middle East can be precarious, and it is palpable in daily life. As an interviewer, you must present yourself as assured and compassionate. I think I learned much of this self-assuredness through public speaking.

Public speaking is vital because it is a skill that bleeds into every part of your life. To be comfortable in front of a group of people is truly a skill that needs to be cultivated; it doesn't just come naturally. It's not simply learning how to say words loudly and clearly but an exercise in presenting yourself from every angle to a variety of different audiences, and being comfortable in your own skin.

I think I will always remember giving my Communication Analysis in the AFA [American Forensic Association] national collegiate speech and debate final in 2011, not because I felt that my performance was remarkable, but I felt as if the round was everything that I love about speech: a group of diverse individuals, presenting topics that they were personally connected to and wanted a broader audience to know about.

A compelling introduction is important because without it you lose your audience—and this is true for all mediums, whether it's in print, video, or public speaking.

When I write for *Al Jazeera*, I always begin with a person's story or a small anecdote that sets the scene. I introduce a character, give personal details, and then I transition into the information and the bulk of the story.

When creating introductions, think of how to make it personal—it's about people, not ideas or facts. Think: if I were watching or reading this, what would make me want to get to the end? Often, it's because we want to find out what happened to the people in the story.

My advice to a new speaker would be to never get defensive, to observe others and look for great speakers to emulate, and to never stop the process of learning. Whether you have been involved in public speaking for 15 years and it is actively part of your daily life, or you have just three months of a course under your belt, you can always learn new things.

It is a craft that is always evolving, always changing, so you must change with it. Above all, be passionate. Be passionate. I wrote that twice because, in my opinion, it is the key to being a great speaker.

Conclusions

Conclusions are incredibly important, though speakers often tend to undervalue them. They will be the parting thought, the last thing an audience remembers. Do them right, and the audience will be sure to talk about your speech afterward.

Conclusions are structured somewhat like introductions, only backwards. Begin with the thesis. Then follow with a review of what you covered before linking back to an AGD that will leave the audience with some memorable thought, cementing a favorable impression of you and your message in their minds.

The following are three AGD ideas that work in conclusions:

- **Quotations make strong conclusions.** While starting your speech with a quotation is not a good idea, ending it with the supportive words of someone who has acquired enough celebrity to warrant quoting can help add to your ethos. The audience will sit up and think, Wow, if David Bowie agrees with her, then she *must* know what she is talking about! You can also quote a surprising source with ironic undertones.

  Using a quotation as a concluding AGD can also be a great way to influence the audience's emotions as you finish speaking. For example, choosing a familiar quotation from a well-known historical figure (Franklin D. Roosevelt) that was given in response to some extraordinary historical occurrence (Pearl Harbor) can be particularly helpful if you want the audience to feel a strong connection to the message. The familiar quotation makes the audience more comfortable, and communicates, "What you just heard is, in fact, something familiar. I just offered my perspective. I encourage you to offer yours."

- **Breaking your speech down to a simple, intuitive message makes for a strong conclusion.** You can use your conclusion to transition from the explanatory or argumentative tone of your speech to a more folksy, relaxed tone. This allows you to step away from the pomp of public speaking or the event at which you are speaking and just communicate. Here's how we might use this technique to end this chapter:

  > Look, we're not saying you have to buy in to all of this introduction and conclusion stuff whole hog. We're just suggesting that you consider the opening and closing of your speech with care.

This is called tonal shift. We used a formal tone advocating the benefits of using well-structured introductions and conclusions throughout the chapter; then we concluded with an informal tone. Perhaps you give a speech encouraging the audience to take a more personal responsibility for the environment. If you ended with a tonal shift, your conclusion might be, "Look, I'm not expecting every member of the audience to race out and buy a car that runs on garbage and peanut butter tomorrow, I'm just saying that if we all just took the first step—like recycling paper in your home—then all of us could immediately contribute toward building a more beautiful and livable Earth."

The important concept to grasp is that you can eliminate the frills and simplify your message at the end of the speech in order to achieve a more holistic persuasive or informative outcome.

- **The great tie-in.** Consider returning to the AGD you used in your introduction. This works best if the speech has taught something that changes the AGD in some way. If your AGD was about a memory, then bring that memory back in the end. Tell us what you learned. If your AGD involved an imaginary conflict with a public figure, then come conclusion time, go ahead and invite that person to dinner. If your AGD used statistics and figures to grab the audience's attention, use figures that represent change.

Finally, avoid using overtly *this is the end* language like, "In conclusion" or "To wrap things up." You don't need these verbal markers to transition to your conclusion; simply move into your conclusion without them.

Tying It Together: Authentic Communication

The barrier between a speaker and an audience is like a door that the speaker wants to walk through. Some people leave their doors wide open, and these audience members are easy to reach. Other audience members keep their doors locked, however. With the AGD, you are trying to get the audience to open their door; once they open it, an effective link, justification, and thesis gets you inside. Your audience receives many messages a day, and as a speaker you are charged with distinguishing yourself from the other messages. Why is your message important? Why should we listen? A strong introduction answers these questions.

Most of us are well aware of the importance of first impressions, but conclusions are just as important. If you've worked so hard to earn your audience's respect through the body of your speech, then don't cheat your work by giving the audience an opportunity to shrug and think, "Whatever," in the end. We know you have something important to share. A strong introduction will make sure your audience listens; a strong conclusion will make sure they remember.

LET'S GIVE A SPEECH

Entrances and Exits

You are the Big Bad Wolf of Fairy Tale Forest, and you must convince the Three Little Pigs to open their door and let you in so you can watch the game on their flat screen. The house is made of brick, so you can't blow it down. You'll have to get in with some top-notch introductions and conclusions. Using the prompts below, brainstorm some arguments and compose introductions that have an AGD, LINK, JUSTIFICATION, THESIS, and PREVIEW; then compose conclusions that use the same material (but in reverse!).

Persuasive	The pigs should go outside to play.
Informative	Watching the game with friends can be very fun.
Speaker's Choice	Murder in Fairy Tale Forest is on the decline.

Key Concepts

- A strong introduction has an AGD, a link, a justification, a thesis, and a preview.

- A strong AGD is interesting, broad, and reinforces the tone and idea of the speech.

- Some common types of AGD include quotations, facts and figures, hypothetical stories, real anecdotes, and fables and allegories.

- A strong link redirects the momentum of the AGD toward the topic of the speech.

- A strong thesis statement includes a justification.

- A preview can help the audience anticipate and follow a speech.

- A strong conclusion mirrors the introduction, starting with the thesis and ending with an AGD.

CHAPTER 9

Physical Delivery

How do you prepare your body for public speaking? For this unit, you will need a new pair of running sneakers, a gym towel, and access to a gymnasium with a bunch of weights. Of course, we're kidding . . . mostly. While you will not necessarily need to visit a shoe store for some new kicks before you begin public speaking, you *will* need to learn some physical skills. It may not be as exhausting as exercise, but it will definitely be worth it.

Excellent public speakers have excellent posture; they use the space around them effectively; they gesture in a powerful and composed way; they maintain meaningful eye contact; and they enhance their message through facial expressions. All of these methods of communication are physical. This chapter will instruct you in each of these skills, and once these physical skills take root in your body, you will be ready to get your body into speaking shape.

Letting Your Body Do the Talking

Whether you are aware of it or not, your body communicates a great deal to others. The way you are sitting at your desk as you are reading this text suggests your level of interest in the material. Are you slouching? Is your head resting on your hands, or is your hand holding the corner of the page, eager to read the next sentence? What you are doing now says something.

We can generally sense when something is wrong with a friend or significant other just by looking at them. Perhaps you see that they are less inclined to look you in the eye, or they seem to shrink away from the world. These physical observations can communicate a great deal about a person. In fact, child developmental psychologists have determined that gestures become sophisticated before children ever learn to speak. Before a child can communicate with words, she learns to reach out in a certain way to say, "Hey, mom, lift me up!" Essentially, we become efficient physical communicators before we become vocal ones.

Thus, understanding how and what our bodies communicate is an essential step in becoming a more proficient speaker. You might be thinking, so if *everything* I'm doing communicates something, how do I possibly stay in control of my message? We'd say the best communicators are in control of every aspect of their performance, but a great place to start is by developing a better command of your posture, gestures, eye contact, and facial expressions.

Posture

Our posture says a lot about our mental and physical state. When we slouch, we communicate to others that we are in a bad mood or that we are physically uncomfortable. Either way, slouching conveys unpleasantness. In contrast, when we stand tall, we communicate that we are happy, strong, and confident.

Some speaking engagements will require you to remain seated, but you can still communicate poise from that position. When the president addresses the nation from the Oval Office, he often does so while seated behind a desk. Whether seated or standing, proper posture communicates self-assurance.

Not only does posture communicate in its own right, it helps the speaker communicate her messages more clearly. Bad posture can inhibit the volume of air in your lungs and force you to breathe from your upper chest. We will discuss why breathing from your chest is bad in the next chapter.

So now that you understand why posture is important, let's talk about ways to improve your posture. When delivering a speech from a standing position, your feet should be less than shoulder width apart. Imagine that there is a string running from your hips all the way through the top of your head. Now picture a celestial being in the sky above you pulling the string taut. Next, take mental note of your shoulders, arms, and hands. Some speakers will stand with their shoulder rolled forward so that their arms face forward with their hands resting on their laps. Don't do that. You'll look like a gorilla. Keep your shoulders rolled back so that your hands rest along the side of your pants seam when you aren't gesturing.

Your head communicates quite a bit, too. Tilting your head up communicates that you are looking down on your audience, like a queen looking down on her subjects. You want to communicate that you are on the same level with your audience. Simply keeping your head level goes a long way to establish common ground. This is called the neutral position.

When speaking from a sitting position, keep your shoulders back, but lean slightly in to your audience. This physically suggests immediacy and comfort. Rest your hands on the desk in front of you. Placing your hands under the desk restricts your ability to gesture comfortably.

POSTURE

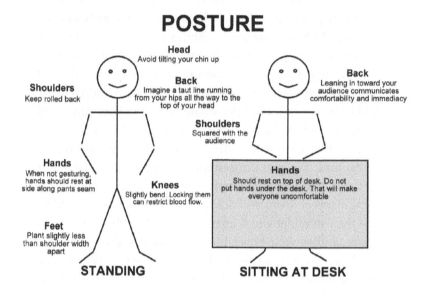

Gestures

"What do I do with my hands?" We hear that a lot in public speaking courses. "My hands look so stupid!" We hear that too. "My arms look like a couple of noodles dangling off the end of a fork." We heard that one once and laughed. Gesturing, like talking, is something we are very good at doing until we are told to do it in a speech. If someone videotaped every great story you've ever told your closest friends and played it back for you, you'd be astonished at how confident and skillful you were at physically expressing yourself.

The use of gestures to communicate ideas is almost instinctive in humans. Early on, we recognize that moving our arms and hands in specific ways can enhance our message. For some, gestures are the only way to communicate. Children born deaf typically struggle to communicate vocally. However, as cognitive neuroscientist Dr. Laura Ann Petitto discovered, deaf children babble with their hands.[1] Just as hearing babies vocalize "da-da" and "ma-ma," deaf children create signs to indicate what they need. As public speakers, we need to channel these instinctive physical movements into refined gestures.

Before we do that, though, we need to have a starting point for our gestures, a position we call *gesture neutral*. In the neutral position, a speaker's arms are relaxed at his sides, and his hands hang naturally beside his thighs. The middle finger of each hand should line up with the pants seam. This is the starting and ending position for every gesture; it is the natural, "home base" position for an effective speaker. At first this position will seem awkward because people usually don't stand like this; we are always fidgeting with something, putting our hands in our pockets, or crossing them in front of or behind our bodies. All of these extra movements or odd alignments can distract from your message, though; so, to let your ideas shine, return to a comfortable gesture-neutral position when possible.

Now that we know what "not-gesturing" looks like, let's talk about gestures, which are movements with a beginning, middle, and an end that emphasize or provide greater clarity to our vocal communication. For example, the phrase, "Look at that" requires a gesture to clarify what you are telling someone to look at. Even when not *necessary,* gestures can still be used to enhance vocal communication. For example, imagine someone saying "We need to act NOW!" If that speaker assertively points to the floor when they say "NOW," the gesture creates a greater sense of urgency to his statement.

Though easy to visualize, effective gesturing can be quite difficult for many speakers. Students often have an especially tough time with the "middle" part of the movement. You've probably seen a great many speakers who move their arms a bit too frantically. In all likelihood, these speakers are skipping the all-important middle, where the gesture and language connect to create a lasting image for the audience.

Excellent public speakers consider the *duration* of the gesture, or how long the action of the gesture is sustained; this is the middle. A great way to understand duration is to think of gestures as a series of statuesque *poses*. That way, you aren't flailing your arms around, but instead, moving from one impactful image to the next.

So if we know that gestures play a part in everyday communication, then how can we use gestures effectively when communicating authentically with a listening audience? We can do so by using two types of gestures: explanatory and expressive.

EXPLANATORY GESTURES

Explanatory gestures are the spontaneous gestures that we typically associate with conversation. If you were introducing your friend Seth, you might say, "This is my friend, Seth." You might also include an explanatory gesture, bending your elbow at approximately 90 degrees and opening your palm toward Seth. You probably have never thought about this gesture in such specific terms, because explanatory gestures are largely instinctual in everyday conversation. Let's take a closer look at some of the most common and useful explanatory gestures.

- **The Offering Gesture**

  When to Use: Use this gesture whenever you introduce a new idea or new information. The gesture says "Consider this."

What It Looks Like: Like you are offering a friend delicate strawberries on a silver plate.

The Breakdown: Starting from neutral, the hand moves forward and outward from the side in a controlled motion. The gesture does not "sweep" outward (like a sideways karate chop) as much as it creates a gentle arc that lands in the offering position. The elbow ends up bent at about 90 degrees, and the hand is open, palm-up, with the fingers forming a stable plane for the plate to rest on. (The fingers shouldn't be curled up or overly tense; try to hold them in a comfortable way that would keep the strawberries from rolling off the plate). Hold the pose; then return to neutral.

- **The Emphasizing Gesture**

When to Use: Use this gesture when you need to emphasize an idea or information. The gesture says "This is important."

What It Looks Like: Like gently placing your fingertips (or fist or pointer) on a table.

The Breakdown: Starting from neutral, the hand or hands move forward from the body, then slightly downward for emphasis. The slight vertical motion at the end of the gesture serves as the focal point. The hand(s) can take many shapes for this gesture (Pres. Bill Clinton preferred to make a fist with the tip of his thumb peeking out; other speakers prefer to point toward the floor), but the most universal form of the gesture is the inverse of the Offering Gesture: hand open, palm-down, with the fingers spread and reaching down to a flat plane. Hold the pose; then return to neutral.

- **The Negative Gesture**

When to Use: Use this gesture to indicate negation, rejection, or denial. The gesture says "No" to or about something.

What It Looks Like: Like you are politely but firmly turning down or refusing to take a strawberry from the plate.

The Breakdown: Starting from neutral, the hand moves forward from the body as if to emphasize information; instead of ending with a slight downward movement, the hand and arm move downward and away from the body, like a slow sideways karate chop. The hand is open, palm-down, and the fingers are spread. After a slight pause at the end of the sideways movement, return to neutral.

- **The Contrast Gesture**

  When to Use: Use this gesture when you have two contrasting ideas in one statement. The gesture says "These things are different."

  What It Looks Like: Like you didn't like what the palm reader had to say, so you deny him the opportunity to read your palm.

  The Breakdown: Starting from neutral, both hands move forward and toward the center of your torso as if to say "Please, sir, I want some more." The elbow ends up bent at about 90 degrees and the hands are open, palm-up. Hold the pose as though you are having your palms read. When you reach a contrasting idea in the sentence, rotate your wrists toward each other until the palm faces the floor. Hold the pose, then return to neutral.

- **The Transitional Gesture**

  When to Use: Use this gesture when you want to physically connect two or more ideas during a preview statement, a list, or any transition. The gesture says "Also, there's this . . . and this . . . and this . . ."

What It Looks Like: When sing-alongs tell you to "follow the bouncy ball!"

The Breakdown: Starting from the neutral position, one hand/arm or both bend at the elbow at approximately 90 degrees. The hands then move across the body from right to left (or left to right), stopping to indicate a new idea or thought. On each new point, the orientation of the palms (either palms up, palms down, or palms perpendicular to the floor) changes.

Speakers can gesture in countless ways to help explain their ideas, and each gesture can have countless minute variations: the angle of the wrist, the orientation of the fingers, and the duration of the pose. These suggestions are only a starting point for building an effective and comfortable repertoire of explanatory gestures that you can deploy in any speaking situation.

EXPRESSIVE GESTURES

Explanatory gestures will work in nearly any context; they are the universal movements of public speaking. The most dynamic speakers, though, go beyond the explanatory into the expressive. Expressive gestures are less instinctual and require more planning. They serve to physically demonstrate a concept or emotion. A speaker might say "I felt like a prisoner" and include an expressive gesture that represents the emotion of imprisonment, like wrapping their arms across their chest or indicating the bars of a jail cell. Such tactics can make the vocal content stand out in the minds of your audience.

Expressive gestures are used in many types of performance. Slam poets use these types of gestures to physically communicate emotional concepts, like freedom, rage, guilt, or love in interesting ways. Many Native American tribes hold storytelling as a central tradition, and storytellers use very specific, dynamic gestures to ensure that young people remember the important aspects of the story. These bolder gestures can make your message last in the minds of your audience. Let's take a look at some ideas or concepts that speakers might communicate and how they can use expressive gestures to do so.

- **Progress**

  When to Use: Use this gesture when you have language that indicates progression or future action. The gesture says "Moving forward. . ."

  What It Looks Like: One hand is pole vaulting over the other.

  The Breakdown: Starting from neutral, both hands move forward and toward the center of your torso. The elbow ends up bent at about 90 degrees, and the hands are perpendicular to the floor. Then move the right hand over the left.

- **Anger**

  When to Use: Use this gesture when you need to express anger or outrage. The gesture says "I am really angry about this."

  What It Looks Like: Like getting ready for a fistfight. Not that we condone fist fighting. Or any kind of fighting.

  The Breakdown: Starting from neutral, the hands and arms move up and inward toward the body; the shoulders are tense and lifted, and the head and neck come slightly forward and down. The hands may form fists or just slightly close. The speaker projects tension and restraint from this position, then returns to neutral.

- **Hope**

  When to Use: Use this gesture when projecting optimism or big, bold ideas. The gesture says "I am excited about the possibilities."

What It Looks Like: An explorer taking in a grand vista.

The Breakdown: Starting from neutral, the chin tilts up, the shoulders push back, and the hands and arms move upward and outward from the body. The hands are palms-up, fingers spread, and the arms slowly sweep outward to take in the entire room. The hands end up closer to shoulder-height than in other gestures, as if they are lifting the spirits of the room.

- **Expansion/Regression**

  When to Use: When you need to indicate growth or regression. The gesture says "This gets bigger (or smaller)."

  What It Looks Like: You are holding a tiny fish that magically grows into a quite large fish, or vice versa.

  The Breakdown: Beginning from neutral position, both hands lift forward and toward the center of the torso. Both hands and elbows then move apart, to show expansion or growth. To show shrinking or regression, the speaker will perform the same gestures in reverse.

Describing effective gestures with words is very difficult, so please know that these breakdowns are a starting point, not the last word, for your expressive gesture repertoire. Stand in front of a mirror, try some of these ideas, and see what looks and feels best for you.

Now that you're feeling more comfortable with movement, we can explore what surrounds movement: space and stillness.

USING SPACE WHEN GESTURING

The space around a speaker is typically rather empty; we rarely speak in tightly packed crowds or in narrow broom closets. Whether presenting on a stage, at the front of a room, or on an elevated podium, speakers have a lot of room around them to fill with their presence. In fact, the performance space is not limited to the space directly around the speaker. The speaker can actually use as much space as can be contained in the room, or even beyond. A solid understanding of how to use that space will make a speaker's gestures much more effective.

We've divided a speaker's space into four gesture zones: personal, near, there, and beyond.

- **Personal gestures are the closest to the body; they actually often point toward or refer to the body.** They are used to represent personal ideas, or they can represent an idea with which the speaker wants to identify. For example, if a speaker says, "We, as Americans, cannot stand for the reelection of Mayor McMaybe," the speaker could gesture to herself when saying "Americans." Other uses of personal gestures could include referring to things she can or could have experienced. For example, a speaker could touch her head when saying "hat," touch her wrist when talking about a watch, or place both hands over her ears when describing pop music featuring auto-tuned teen vocalists. Personal gestures invite the audience to share in the speaker's experience; they are powerful and intimate.

- **Near gestures reference the space between the shoulders (in front of the body) or just outside the shoulders (within a foot or so of the speaker's sides).** These gestures can describe the space near a speaker, or they can represent ideas that the speaker is comfortable with, but may not necessarily identify with personally. To take the earlier example, the speaker could say, "Many Americans oppose the reelection of Mayor McMaybe," while presenting an offering gesture near her body. This indicates that she is sympathetic to those Americans, but may not be one of them. Near gestures are somewhat more objective than personal gestures, although they can still indicate support or understanding.

- **There gestures are within arm's reach, but distinctly removed from the personal space of the speaker.** These gestures can be used to establish contrast with ideas indicated by a near gesture. For instance, our speaker might say "Mayor McMaybe has many opponents, and they outnumber his supporters," using a near gesture to indicate opponents and a there gesture to indicate supporters. This demonstrates contrast and also reinforces the speaker's sympathies (opponents of Mayor McMaybe are close to the speaker, supporters of Mayor McMaybe are different and further away). These different gesture zones are useful for illustrations and to subtly enhance the speaker's message.

- **Beyond gestures reference ideas or things outside the boundaries of the room; they frequently involve a pointing finger or an open hand flung toward the horizon.** These are often the biggest, most dynamic gestures in a speech. Consider our example. If the speaker were to say, "Maybe in some communist dystopia they would elect Mayor McMaybe, but not here in America," she could use a pointy beyond gesture when saying, "communist dystopia." The beyond gesture need not be negative, however; it can indicate any framework, existence, idea, faction, entity, culture, or realm that exists "somewhere else." For example, if a community organizer says, "Let's go out there and show the world what we can accomplish when we work together," he could use the beyond gesture when saying "the world."

USING STILLNESS WHEN GESTURING

Using the space around us is important; dynamic gestures can broaden our impact and enhance our message. But gesturing non-stop can become a distraction (and tire you out). Stillness is an important component of physical performance not only because it breaks up the stream of gestures, but also because it, in itself, is a powerful gesture.

Remember that gestures are movements with a beginning, middle, and an end. Well, what should you do before the beginning and after the ending of your gesture? Just stand there. Be comfortable in that gesture neutral position. Stand tall with your hands resting comfortably at your sides until you reach a moment in your speech that requires physical expression; then begin the gesture.

Keep in mind that knowing when to end a gesture can be just as important as knowing when to begin it. In fact, putting your hands down *is* a gesture, and depending on your precision and commitment, can be a powerful one. When the hands return to neutral at the conclusion of a gesture, the audience's attention is naturally drawn back to the speaker's face and words. Ending a gesture can draw attention to an impactful line in your presentation, so when you want an audience to listen in a focused way, put your hands down.

Eye Contact

Our eyes also communicate a great deal to others. When we roll our eyes, we signal that we disagree with our curfew. When our eyes are filled with tears, people assume we have recently cut an onion, our finger, or ties with a boyfriend. Since your eyes communicate so much about your emotional state, how you use eye contact is critical to how your message is received.

When speaking to a large audience, the eye contact method to which most people instinctively default is *the scan*. The scan is when the speaker tries to make eye contact with everyone in the room. The scanner speaks—and scans to the left. Continues speaking—and scans to the right. This pattern is fine for a lawn sprinkler, but it's not good for speakers.

Realistically, a speaker can communicate authentically with only about 15 people during a speaking engagement. So, even if you tried, you can't get to them all. We communicate best when communicating with one audience member at a time, and when we do that, we actually communicate more authentically with the rest of the audience.

If you are speaking to an audience of only 15 people, is it ok to scan? Nope! Making eye contact with one person is more inclusive than trying to make eye contact with everyone. When a speaker scans, no authentic connection happens, so the audience easily loses interest and starts thinking about what they need to pick up for dinner. However, if you make an authentic connection with just one person, and you are not concerned with trying to get to everyone, the entire room feeds off of that one connection. Speaking to *only* one person throughout the engagement will not work, however. Make sustained, meaningful eye contact with individuals. If you connect with individuals throughout your speech, you *will* get to everyone. They will all feel your connection.

Think about your favorite boy band. When they are singing for tens of thousands of people, they narrow their focus. The lead singer will hold the mic in one hand and point to a screaming member of the audience with the other. Then the singer will serenade that person for several lines. He knows that if he is going to communicate with the tens of thousands of people, it will be through one person at a time.

Move Your Face

Speakers have a hard time using facial ges-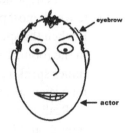
tures because they are not as aware of their
faces as they are their hands and feet. It's easy
to look down and see if you hand is moving
too much or too little, or if you are holding
it too high or low. You can also look down to
adjust the width between your legs, or notice
if your legs are locked or are bent comfort-
ably. But as speakers, we cannot see our faces. Because facial
gestures remain unseen, we need to focus extra attention on
training our faces to make sure that they are communicating
exactly what we want. We're going to look at a few basic facial
expressions and explain how you can produce them letting
Cartoon Jack help us show you what we mean.

Below, you'll have a chance to practice some basic facial
expressions along with Jack. We will focus on your eyebrows
and mouth; these two components can communicate most of
what you want to your audience.

FACED!
starring Cartoon Jack

Begin by practicing in the mirror. See what gestures your face
is capable of making.

Happy Jack
Happy Jack's eyebrows have taken on a
slight angle. They are raised from the cen-
ter of the forehead. Raised eyebrows can
send a powerful message conveying a distinct willingness to communicate and also
reinforce that the speaker is delighted to

---

deliver the speech. Smiling also goes a long way to put the audience at ease. This face is complementary to the audience.

Sad Jack

Sad Jack's eyebrows are relaxed on the top and slightly rounded in the corners as if they are trying to keep from crying. When talking about something sad or unfortunate, it is important that your eyes and mouth communicate empathy toward the subject. Use the Sad Jack face to deliver potentially heartbreaking impact.

Intense Jack

Intense Jack eyebrows are pulled taut from the edges of the brow. The mouth is emotionless, because he is way too intense for silly emotions. Use the Intense Jack face when imploring the audience to take action.

What did you notice? Were any of the faces particularly difficult for you? Note how each face is defined not just by a smile, or lack thereof, but is a composition of parts. It's fine if you do not have 45-degree eyebrows, but it is important to understand the power of eyebrows. A quick-start method to better face gestures is simply to raise and lower your eyebrows. Once we encountered a student who was consistently accused of appearing nasty and uncaring. We simply had him occasionally move his eyebrows up and down while he spoke. He looked silly at first, but his audiences were immediately responsive. They felt he was someone who was interested and excited to speak to them.

A speaker has tremendous power to manipulate how her audience feels about her topic, whether by gesturing with her body or simply moving her eyebrows. Understanding this power is a step closer to harnessing it. The next step is understanding that your face muscles can be trained. If you feel like your smile is forced and awkward, then practice smiling in the mirror. Yes, we are asking you to awkwardly smile in the mirror; but reflecting (literally) on your face gestures is the best way to improve them. Practice: the mirror is your friend. Take control of your face. It is just as important as your arms and legs.

Physical Delivery Using Limited Notes

When the president of the United States addresses the nation, he (or perhaps, someday she) gets to read from a teleprompter. The text rolls in front of the cameras, creating the impression that the president is looking you directly in the eye. The president gestures with compelling fluidity, unbridled and free. Unfortunately, you will not have the luxury of a teleprompter when you deliver your speech; you probably will be using limited notes. So how do you deliver presidential-looking performances under these conditions? Notes can definitely be helpful, but you will need to consider a few points so they do not negatively impact your physical performance.

- **Avoid drawing attention to your notes.** This is your primary goal. You want your hand gestures, eye contact, and facial expression to be so compelling that the audience forgets you are speaking from notes. Creating this illusion is particularly difficult if you read from your notes.

Avoid putting whole sentences from your speech on your notecard. Notes should be used to remind you of your next point and make it easier to recount sources. The less you have written on the card, the less likely you are to find yourself dependent on its contents.

- **Maintain eye contact.** Keeping your notes concise will prevent you from staring down at your notecard and encourage you to practice sustained eye contact. When you do need to use your notes, hold them high so that you can look down and then up without moving your neck. Moving your head up and down distracts from the connection with your audience, and also disrupts your speaking fluency.

- **Keep in mind that using notes will impact your gestures.** Again, your goal is to avoid drawing attention to your notes. When holding a notecard, conceal it in the palm of your hand so your audience will not be distracted. When you need to look at your notes, bend your elbow at 90 degrees or more so you can view the card comfortably. Avoid turning your chin too far toward the floor. You want the sound of your voice to travel out toward your audience and not down toward your feet. If you are speaking from a notepad, be careful not to bounce the pad up and down while you are reading from it. If you need to read from your notepad (to read a long quotation, for example), keep the pad raised until you no longer need it. Effective use of notes is a skill that takes time to develop and, like everything else, requires practice.

Power Posing

We've noted how incorporating gestures and using limited notes can increase the speaker's credibility and the reception of his message. However, social psychologist and Harvard Business School associate professor Amy Cuddy discovered in her research that our physical presence, specifically making ourselves appear physically larger than we are, can change not only how others perceive us but also how we perceive ourselves. Her research focuses primarily on how people judge others. In particular, Cuddy is interested in power dynamics. She explained in a June, 2012, Ted Talk[2] that animals and humans communicate power by taking up large amounts of space. Alpha male gorillas puff up their chests and sit with their arms wide open. Cobras expand their hoods when they are threatened.

Humans also expand when they communicate power, according to Cuddy. Imagine a CEO sitting on a large leather chair with feet on the desk and arms around the head. Doesn't she look powerful? You didn't expect me to say "she," did you? Cuddy observed that women in the Harvard Business School would perform just as well as their male peers on tests but would perform significantly worse in class discussions. In her presentation, Cuddy remarked that women, particularly girls, are taught to take up less space than men. It turns out that this insight into the different ways that men and women are taught to communicate can help speakers of both genders become more powerful communicators.[3]

Cuddy wondered if speakers who faked *looking* powerful would actually *feel* more powerful. As it turns out, they do. Cuddy had one set of participants pose for two minutes in powerless positions, sitting with their shoulders turned in and hands folded. She had another set "Power Pose" for two minutes. These students took on positions that expanded their arms and puffed out their chest. Then she took saliva samples from both groups. Remarkably, the participants who Power

Posed had significantly higher levels of testosterone (the power hormone) and significantly lower levels of cortisol (the stress hormone).[4]

Cuddy's research tells us two things. First, it's a good idea to power pose for a couple of minutes (away from others) before you give a presentation. The research suggests that doing so makes you more confident and less stressed. Second, this research also reminds us of the importance of opening up your physicality. Stand tall, don't shy away from bigger gestures, take up space, and be *powerful*.

SPEAKER SPOTLIGHT

Lanna Joffrey
Actor

Lanna Joffrey is an actor, writer, spoken word performer, teacher, coach, and student. She received a NY International Fringe Festival Performance Award for her work in VALIANT, her original documentary play of women's war stories. She treats each public speaking opportunity as a gift, and knows that there is power in the spoken word.

I love words and the arrangement of words. I love hearing something I didn't know.

I am drawn to shy people because maybe they know the secret to life. I do not know the secret to life so I can't stop speaking and discussing.

I spend a large portion of my life creating work that will be publicly heard in hopes of shaking and shifting paradigms for the better.

The opportunity to speak publicly is a gift. Millions of people are never given this gift. They are not allowed to speak and share their personal thoughts. Men and women are silenced on a daily basis throughout the world, so cherish this gift. With this gift say something of worth.

Public speaking is essentially about the quantity of ears hearing your out-loud thoughts.

Say something you are compelled by. Say something you are passionate about. Speak for yourself. Speak for those who cannot speak, for those who are forbidden to speak. Speak publicly and be grateful for it.

Where to Stand

Where you are in relation to your audience is important to their reception of your message. Reflect on some of the best speakers you've encountered. Think about your teachers: Were the best teachers those that lecture from one place, maybe hidden behind a podium? Or were they the ones who move dynamically in front of (and through) the classroom? Students, like any audience, tend to respond better to the second type of speaker because our proximity to the speaker influences how we receive and interpret her message.

Cultural anthropologist Edward T. Hall refers to this phenomenon as proxemics.[5] He argued that the use of space has a profound influence on interpersonal communication. Someone standing too close to us can make us uncomfortable, especially if we do not have a strong relationship to that person. In the same way, if you are standing too far away from a good friend, she might think you were avoiding her. These spaces vary with culture, but there still seem to be certain universal characteristics.

Hall delineated interpersonal space into four distinct distances:

- **Intimate distance**: This is the space, between 0 and 6 inches from our bodies, that we reserve only for those with whom we maintain an intimate relationship. When you hug your best friend or when you give your mother a kiss, you are inviting them into your intimate space. The reason why we are so uncomfortable with "close talking" strangers is because they are invading a space we normally reserve for close friends and loved ones.

- **Personal distance**: This is the space, about 6 inches to 4 feet from our bodies, into which we typically speak with friends and family. It's not quite intimate, but it's comfortable.

- **Social distance**: This is the space, between 4 and 10 feet from our bodies, reserved for acquaintances, or people we've just met.

- **Public distance**: This is the distance—which Hall believed is beyond 10 feet—that we typically associate with public speeches.

So how do we apply this understanding of space to your speaking? Before you speak in front of an audience, examine the architecture of the room. A classroom generally has about 5 to 10 feet of space between the front wall and the first row of desks. This puts you within "social distance" from your audience. That's a good thing. Remember, our goal is authentic communication. Standing about 4 to 6 feet from your audience will communicate that you are comfortable inviting them into your social space. If you can't get that close, try to remove obstacles between you and your audience; step out from behind a podium, or come out from behind that table.

Your audience may not be uniformly distributed through-out the room. For some reason, everyone in class decided to bunch together on the left side of the room, leaving the right side deserted. What do you do? You want to avoid creating negative space. In art, the negative space refers to the space around the subject. As speakers, we are like the subject of a painting. We want our audience to look at us, not the space surrounding us. Therefore, you want to center yourself to the audience, not the architecture of the room. So, if everyone is sitting to the left, center yourself accordingly.

Walking

We have all seen them. Public speakers who pace back and forth in front of the room while they speak. Pacers are a lot like the speakers we discussed earlier who scan the audience. They have the right idea (they know it's important to use space) but don't know how to execute it effectively. To understand how to confidently and appropriately use space, you have to use walking to your advantage.

Walking works best when it serves a purpose. Think about it this way: when you walk in daily life, you usually have some reason for doing so. If you are thirsty, you walk over to the cupboard to grab a glass, then walk over to the sink to fill the glass with water. In daily life, we usually pace only to relieve frustrations.

When you speak, the audience will look for the purpose in your movement. The clearest purpose for walking in speeches is to signal a transition from one point to another. This is known as *physical signposting*. Begin the introduction of your speech with your body centered to your audience. When you transition to the first point, walk to one side of the audience.

When you transition to your second point, move to the other side. This will signal that you are addressing a new subject.

Now that we know when to walk, let's consider how to walk. Some speakers have a tendency to turn their body to the right or left so that the audience sees them in profile. In a move that resembles a drill sergeant, they turn their face away from the audience and toward the direction of their movement. This disrupts the speaker's connection with the audience as it severs eye contact and gives the physical impression of alienation. Don't give your audience "the cold shoulder!"

Instead, turn your shoulders and head toward your audience when you walk. Connect with a person at the end of the room you are walking toward. For example, if you will be delivering your first point to the right side of your audience, look to a person sitting on the far right side before you walk in that direction. Walk at a pace that reflects the tone and rate of your speech. This will ensure that your physical transitions are confident and smooth.

Tying It Together: Authentic Communication

Delivering a speech is a physically demanding activity. And just like playing a musical instrument or a sport, public speaking requires practice. Physical practice. So get in shape. Use a mirror. Video yourself and study the film. Analyze how you use eye contact, gestures, and posture.

When you perfect your physical presentation, your confidence will soar, and this will be reflected in your vocal performance and the reaction of your audience. A speaker who is comfortable in his own body makes the audience comfortable in their seats; a physically awkward performance is difficult to watch, and even more difficult to connect with.

Authentic communication is physical, vocal, and mental; keep all three in mind as you progress as a speaker.

Isolating and Understanding Physical Delivery

The purpose of this exercise is to become more aware of our physical choices. Using a speech composed in an earlier chapter, deliver the first three sentences to a mirror, observing your physical delivery. Then follow these steps to better understand the power of physical delivery.

Step 1: Body Consciousness.
Looking at your body as you speak, answer these questions.

Shoulders and Neck	How high is your chin? Pointed toward your chest? The ceiling? The back wall?
	Is your neck straight or curved?
	Are your shoulders tense or relaxed?
Arms and Hands	Where are your arms? Hanging at your side? Slightly in front of your body? Behind?
	Are your hands loose or tight? Are your fingers curled or straight?
Legs and Feet	Are your feet parallel?
	Are your legs straight or bent?
	Are your hips over your knees, or are you jutting one hip out as you speak?

Step 2: Improving Your Delivery, One Body Part at a Time.
Use these guidelines to arrange your body for maximum speaking potential.

Shoulders and Neck	Pretend a string is attached to the top of your head and is holding you up.
	Lift your chest up as you roll your shoulders back.
	The goal is to stand as tall as you comfortably can. Do not budge from your superior height. Deliver your speech with power.
Arms and Hands	In your neutral position, your arms should rest comfortably at your sides.
	Some speakers tend to rest their arms in front of their torso (nearly touching the thigh).
	Your hands should be positioned beside the widest parts of your hips or thighs (or your pants seam).
Legs and Feet	Your feet should be just inside shoulder-width.
	Your weight should be distributed evenly on both legs.

Step 3: Make Your Muscles Remember.
Deliver your speech again, in full, maintaining whatever adjustments you made in Step 2. Insist on proper physical delivery whenever you speak or practice. Through repetition, your body will acclimate to this posture and you will be able to focus on your verbal and vocal delivery.

Key Concepts

- Humans communicate as much physically as vocally, so physical delivery is important to master.

- Upright, stable posture enhances communication.

- Both explanatory and expressive gestures can be effective, as can neutral gestures, or stillness.

- Eye contact is best when it is sustained, meaningful, and focused on a few audience members.

- Speakers can communicate emotion and intensity with their faces.

- Effective speakers understand and use space to their advantage by positioning themselves appropriately in relation to their audiences and the layout of the speech venue.

CHAPTER 10

Vocal Delivery

Most of the time, we don't think about our voices. We go about our daily lives vocally uninhibited, telling jokes, sharing secrets, trading details about our weekend without ever having to think about how our voices work. When we speak to our friends, we don't think about the intricate mechanical process of sound production and manipulation that is occurring as we speak. But just speaking doesn't produce effective public speakers. We need to think about vocal delivery, understand it, and practice it.

How Does Speaking Work?

When we want to say something, our lungs take in air. The amount of air they take in depends on the type of sound we wish to produce. For example, it takes a lot more breath to shout across a track field or yell at your sibling at the other side of the house than it does to ask the student in front of you to borrow a pen. The air in our lungs gives us pressure to vibrate our vocal folds (or vocal cords). Our vocal folds are the two membranes that control the airflow. The muscles in our larynx stretch our vocal folds to reach an appropriate tone and pitch. Our articulatory tools (lips, cheeks, palate, teeth, and tongue) manipulate the sound.

Your body does this process naturally, without pause, all the time. That is, until you get in front of an audience, when nervousness gets a hold of you and your adrenaline shoots up to compensate for all of the anxiety. You become a stuttering mess of incoherent vowels and half-eaten words. In that moment, well-planned breathing can save you; haphazard breathing can destroy your presentation.

Proper breathing is the absolute first step in good vocal delivery. All the areas of vocal delivery we will discuss later depend on proper breathing, so we will take some extra time now to explain how to optimize your breath.

WHY PLANNED BREATHING IS IMPORTANT

Haphazard breathing results in two problems: warped tone and uneven energy. Tone is the first thing that audiences notice. A strong, controlled tone communicates a strong speaker, one the audience will trust. A shaky, uncontrolled tone communicates a weaker speaker, one the audience worries for, creating a shared anxiety. The latter is extremely common, even for typically confident people. We hear it all the time on television when people are speaking to a live audience: An uneasy beginning, a slight quiver in the voice. Most people think the solution to a shaky tone is just for the performer not to be so nervous. But how on earth can you tell your body not to be nervous? The shakiness in the vocal delivery is the result of uneven breath. So, the answer?: Breath, breathing, planned breathing.

The second way breath betrays the speaker is through uneven energy. Sometimes a speaker will begin confidently but will lose some of her energy and confident volume as her speech progresses; as a result, the audience will start to lose interest. But planned breathing can solve this problem, too.

DON'T BREATHE WITH YOUR CHEST

It all starts with air. Go ahead, breathe in some air. As you breathe in, focus on where the air goes in your body; feel your chest expand as your lungs fill. Maybe your stomach expands, also. Which filled first? Did your stomach expand first, then the lungs, or did your chest expand but not your stomach? The latter is a sign that you may be chest breathing. Chest breathing is that kind of breathing people do when someone commands them to "take a deep breath." They suck in air with a big "heeennnnhhh" sound, their chest gets big and puffy, their jaw clenches up and their neck juts out. Chest breathing is bad because it doesn't enable you to maximize your airflow. So how should you breathe? With your diaphragm.

BREATHE WITH YOUR DIAPHRAGM

The lungs don't actually draw air into themselves. Instead, air is drawn into the lungs by the contraction of the diaphragm, a sheet-looking muscle that separates the chest cavity from the abdominal cavity. When the diaphragm is relaxed, it rests against the bottom of the lungs like a dome; when it is flexed, it pushes outward and downward, expanding the abdominal cavity and creating a vacuum in the lungs. This action is what draws air into the chest. If the stomach stays drawn in, the diaphragm can't expand fully, limiting the amount of air pulled into the lungs. By expanding your stomach, you are literally creating more room in your chest cavity for air to flow into the lungs.

Consequently, a speaker's posture is important to facilitate full breathing. If the speaker is hunched over, jutting his hip to one side, or otherwise constricting his abdominal and chest cavities, he is limiting the amount of air that he can use when speaking. Posture is important for a variety of perceptual reasons, but at the very least a speaker needs to find a comfortable, "tall" posture that facilitates powerful speaking.

A Guide to Better Breathing

1. Begin by taking in a comfortable amount of air.

2. On the exhale, make an "ahh" sound as loudly and as long as you comfortably can. Don't shriek; just make a completely neutral "ahhh." Think relaxing in a hot tub "ahh," not an "I got startled by a clown 'AH!'" Hold the sound until all the air is out of your lungs and take another breath.

3. Are your shoulders going up more than your belly is sticking out? You are probably breathing from your chest rather than your diaphragm. That's okay, the next step will help! To practice diaphragmatic breathing, place your hand on your belly while standing up, or lie down and place a book on your abdomen. Take in a deep breath, pushing your hand out or the book up.

4. While taking a full abdominal breath, release, making the same "ahh" sound as loudly and as long as you comfortably can. Notice a difference? The sound should be much louder and longer than before.

---

5. Continue practicing taking full diaphragmatic breaths. Lightheadedness is a temporary side effect of this exercise. Practicing diaphragmatic breathing gives your body more oxygen than it may be used to, but breathing from your diaphragm will eventually become second nature.

GOOD VIBRATIONS

Now that you know how to breathe, let's examine how you produce sound. As we exhale, air is expelled from the lungs and through the vocal folds, or vocal cords. The vocal cords are stretched or relaxed by the muscles of the larynx, and they vibrate as the air from the lungs passes through them. These vibrations generate sound waves, which make up the majority of the sound we craft into words. It's important to remember that the sound—and power—of your voice actually originates in the lungs and larynx, not in the mouth; picturing the voice originating in this way can help reduce unneeded strain in a lot of speakers.

Once the sound is flowing, the speaker shapes the sound into words, a job for the articulatory tools: the lips, the cheeks, the teeth, palate, and the tongue. Let's look at how to get the most out of this process.

How to Speak Better

As we just detailed, speaking is a complex process, involving many moving parts; the vocal product that speakers generate can be rich or poor, nuanced or flat, powerful or underwhelming. It all depends on how it's prepared. Every voice is different, and every speech calls for a unique vocal style.

We like to think about vocal delivery as a checklist. The first and most basic concern is just being heard, which means producing an appropriate level of volume. After a speaker is projecting well, we concern ourselves with how fast she is talking; the speech needs to be delivered at a rate that the audience can follow. Of course, speaking at an acceptable rate is useless without speaking clearly, so speakers must articulate their words. Finally, once these more mechanical issues are settled, the speaker must seek ways to enhance the impact of her words; she must use appropriate tone and pitch.

Each of these considerations contributes to the overall vocal delivery, and when they work in concert it can be a beautiful thing.

CAN THE AUDIENCE HEAR YOU? THINKING ABOUT VOLUME AND PROJECTION

Volume is useful to be heard, but it's also an important persuasive tool. The volume of our voice is primarily related to the amount of air we expel, and the rate at which we expel it. Do it loudly enough to be heard in every corner.

Other than to be heard, there are a few ways to use variations in volume to your advantage.

- **Match your volume to your room.** Take care to adjust your volume to your space. You would speak at a different volume entirely if you were exchanging pleasantries with a friend in the privacy and confines of a broom closet than if you were saying hello to that same friend from across a noisy gym during basketball practice.

A good way to adjust your volume is to visualize the audience lined up along the rear of the room; you want to speak just loudly enough that they can comfortably hear you. Don't speak to just the front row, and don't yell to the corridor. Push your voice to the rear and back.

It's a good idea to practice your projection before you get up to speak. If you are speaking in your classroom, sit in the back of class one day and ask or respond to a teacher's question to make sure you are projecting adequately. If you are delivering in a space you are unfamiliar with, arrive with a friend before your audience shows up and test whether or not your friend can hear you when she stands in the back of the room. Keep in mind that the more people you add to a given space, with their coughing and shifting, the more loudly you'll need to project.

- **Use your dynamic range.** Some people will tell you that being loud is the best way to emphasize a point; others advise speaking softly. They're both right, and they're both wrong. But first, some science.

  The human brain is remarkably adept at ignoring things. Stare at a spot on the wall long enough and it disappears; sit in a musty room long enough and you forget the smell. The brain is very good at filtering out steady sensory input; we get desensitized very easily. This is why a speaker who emphasizes everything is really emphasizing nothing; the brain just gets used to it.

  If you are really loud throughout your speech, or really quiet, the audience will tire easily. You need to use variations in volume sparingly; a moment or two of gradually developed loudness will have greater effect than a constant barrage of screaming. The *change* in volume is producing the effect. This is why speaking loudly or softly can both be effective—if you change your volume, the audience will notice the change and pay attention.

- **Plan ahead to maximize impact (and use volume appropriately).** In order to plan their breathing for concerts, vocalists mark their music with breath marks. This is called scoring a script. The vocalist might strike a line through his music for a breath or draw an ascending diagonal line when he wants to remind himself to get louder. This practice can also be a tremendous help when rehearsing a speech. One of the biggest benefits to this methodology is that you can plan your breath. Maybe you want to say a certain three sentences rapidly. In order to do so, you can prepare your breaths so that choice won't impair your energy further into the speech. Also, rehearsing with planned breaths will make sure you are breathing if your body does seize up due to anxiety while speaking. Those breaths will get you out of a jam. They keep the machine moving, making sure all the rehearsal you've done hasn't gone to waste.

Additionally, scoring a script can help shape the dynamics of a speech, just as a vocalist marks a score to shape dynamics in a singing performance. Check out the example below. It helps to double-space—or even triple-space—your script to leave room for scoring; if you are using an outline instead of a complete script, you can still score the performance ahead of time. You can make up your own legend or symbols. These symbols make sense to us.

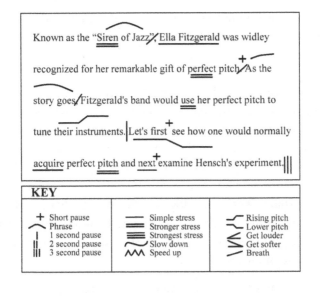

Known as the "Siren of Jazz", Ella Fitzgerald was widley

recognized for her remarkable gift of perfect pitch. As the

story goes, Fitzgerald's band would use her perfect pitch to

tune their instruments. Let's first see how one would normally

acquire perfect pitch and next examine Hensch's experiment.

KEY

+ Short pause	── Simple stress	⌒ Rising pitch
⌢ Phrase	══ Stronger stress	⌒ Lower pitch
ǀ 1 second pause	≡ Strongest stress	⋜ Get louder
ǁ 2 second pause	∿ Slow down	⋝ Get softer
ǀǀǀ 3 second pause	⋀⋀ Speed up	⌒ Breath

THINKING ABOUT TEMPO AND PACE

Oscar, Golden Globe, and Emmy award-winning screenwriter
Aaron Sorkin is known for crafting characters who seem per-
petually under a time crunch. On *The Newsroom*, for example,
his characters are under intense pressure to accomplish tasks.
Sorkin suggests urgency by showing the characters engage in
unusually fast-paced dialogue. As crises resolve themselves
near the end of the episode, the tempo of the dialogue slows
down. This contrasting shift forces the audience to pay attention and usually creates a gripping emotional moment.

What we can learn from Sorkin is that our pace, or the
speed at which we speak, plays a major role in how the audience receives our message. Changes in our pace or tempo can
strike an emotional chord in our audience.

Here are some basic guidelines for tempo and pace that every speaker should follow, and some helpful tricks to maximize your impact as a speaker.

- **Slow down.** Public speaking is exciting, and even the most experienced speakers still get a jolt of anxiety when they address an audience. The most common (nearly universal, in fact) way that this anxiety manifests itself is through elevated tempo. You get nervous, and you subconsciously (or consciously) want to finish your speech as quickly as possible. Even at a biological level, your body will respond to excitement with an elevated heart rate and faster breathing, and this can produce a faster delivery. To counteract these impulses, slow down.

  Remember that your audience will be hearing your speech for the first time. You may be intimately familiar with your topic, but your audience is not; so, you have to give them time to process the information you are presenting.

  This point is worth emphasizing. Not only is your audience hearing your speech for the first time, but they also don't get a chance to review the information as it's coming at them. Hopefully, you've adapted your writing and speech preparation to a listening audience, keeping in mind that, unlike a reading audience, they can't adapt the pace with which they receive the information or go back and reread anything. Still, delivering your speech at a rapid pace will undo any positive adaptation you've made.

  One interesting exercise is to try to speak so slowly that it's almost comical. Once you feel like you are speaking too slowly, you are probably speaking at an acceptable rate. What feels absurdly slow to our excited brains sounds just right to the audience.

- **Use your dynamic range (again).** You've probably had this experience: you are sitting in a lecture or meeting, listening to a professor or colleague drone on about frog biology or spreadsheet security or whatever, and your attention begins to drift. Suddenly, the room goes silent and you wake up and snap back to attention, worried that you've been asked a question and now everyone is waiting for your answer.

  You snap-to because whoever was talking changed their pace. They went from quick, steady talking to sudden silence or slowness, and the change forced your brain back to attention. As with volume, changes in pace produce big effects on an audience. A series of quickly delivered sentences followed by a slow one, or vice versa, can perk up an audience. Work at varying your pace and rate to keep audience interest at peak levels.

- **Think about the different aspects of speed: within words, between words, and between ideas.** Varying *where* you slow down in your speech will ensure that you are both understood and dynamic!

  Varying rate within words: Sometimes speakers say each individual word so quickly and sharply that the words are not clearly heard. Even if they add pauses between the words, the words themselves are not given enough time to "land" or register with the audience. Some words in your speech may be difficult to understand or difficult for you to say, which may be a good time to slow your delivery. Additionally, you can give some of the powerful language in your performance added punch by stretching out the tempo of the words a bit.

  Example: Weee can make a difference.

Elongating the word "we" can make the speech sound more impassioned.

Varying rate between words: Varying the rate between words can also alter how the audience receives your message. You hear politicians utilize this strategy when they give important speeches.

> *Example:* We. . .will. . .not. . .negotiate with terrorists.

With this approach, the speaker adds space between each word, making each sound important.

Varying rate between ideas: Matching an appropriate pace to the emotional context of an idea plays a large role in how the idea is received. During a speech, you will likely have to show different emotions to match what you have composed. Even eulogies often include lighthearted moments about the person's life before shifting toward a more serious reflection of the loss. Changing your rate between these ideas can smooth the emotional transition.

> *Example:* (Casual/natural speaking rate) Anyone who knew Joe, knew he loved to make people laugh. (Slow down the rate *between* the words) So today, we will not mourn his death. . . (Slow down the rate *within* the words, but elongating the word 'celebrate') . . . but celebrate his life.

When practicing your speech, make specific choices about *when* and *how* you'll slow things down.

- **Slow down when you preview or review ideas.** If the audience does not hear and process your preview, they will struggle to follow your logic. The beginnings and ends of your points are also a great place to reset, in case the performance is heading toward the "I'm just going to get this over with" territory. Don't be that person. You've worked really hard on this. Relax, pump the breaks, and reconnect.

Dante Lima
Copywriter and Musician

Dante Lima is a copywriter for Pearson Online Learning Services. He has also worked in journalism, public relations, and the music industry, and recently he began recording his first solo album. He loves his wife, his dog, his guitars, and his golf clubs, in that order. As a creative writer, and particularly as a singer and musician, Dante has some terrific insights into finding your best voice.

I make my living communicating, through both spoken and written word.

Every day I have to find a way to take the concepts that I've created and written and explain them to clients and other professionals, some of whom may be far removed from the process.

When love is injected into a speech, words tend to stick with you.

Clear and confident public speaking says a lot about a person. It demonstrates qualities far beyond the material.

As a singer or speaker, my main focus when I'm performing is to stay within myself. The moment it feels unnatural or affected, I go back to the drawing board.

Great public speakers prepare, and immediately distinguish themselves in a group. These traits translate well to the professional world, but also help you shape your identity in life.

Wedding speeches require the most thought, the most love, and the most bravery to execute. It's the purest form of public speaking I've come across: person to person, yet completely open.

Find the balance between personality and purpose. Every time you speak in public, your speech should have an outcome. But don't forget that the most endearing speakers don't hide from themselves. It's a hard thing to do, even if you don't fear it.

Never forget the value words hold. It's wise not to waste them.

If you aren't staying true to your voice and your abilities, it just turns into bad karaoke.

THINKING ABOUT ARTICULATION AND PRONUNCIATION

Ifhuar spking loully nufand atarate thathaudence cn flow, yar prolly inna gooplace.

Wait, what? Sorry, let's try again.

You may be speaking loudly enough and at a rate that the audience can follow, but if the audience can't understand your words, if you don't articulate properly, your speech will fail. Articulating can be especially tricky because we tend to be very relaxed when we speak casually; our words tumble out with very little emphasis, and we substitute informal pronunciations for formal ones (for example, "gonna" instead of "going to," "prolly" instead of "probably"). In a public speaking setting, we must ramp up our effort. The acoustic dynamics of a big room, the variation among listeners, and the importance or freshness of your ideas all make clear articulation more important.

Here are some tips and tricks to improve your articulation.

- **Warm up your face.** There are lots of ways to get your face ready to articulate properly. Begin by opening your mouth as wide as possible, like you are simulating a yawn. Then bring your lips together and scrunch up your face as tightly as you can, like you are eating a sour candy. Repeat this process a few times, exaggerating the stretch a little more each time.

  It's also helpful to place both hands on your face. Open your mouth and let your hands slide down your cheeks. This should help stretch the jaw.

- **Warm up your tongue.** Your tongue is a big muscle, and like any muscle, it should be warmed up before exercise. As goofy as they may sound, tongue twisters are a great way to do just that.

Sample Tongue Twisters

Here are some sample tongue twisters for you to try; there are longer versions for some of these, just try Googling them.

Peter Piper picked a peck of pickled peppers.

Sally sells sea shells by the sea shore.

Fuzzy Wuzzy was a bear, Fuzzy Wuzzy had no hair.

Enrique makes monstrously bad decisions.

Elizabeth stole my Camaro.

Darius finished the peanut butter and left the refrigerator door open again. Come on, Darius.

- **Strengthen the muscles.** When rehearsing, focus on your enunciation. Sometimes, just thinking about your mouth moving is enough to make your lips work harder. If your mouth is a little sore after rehearsal, don't worry. Your mouth is made up of muscles, and those muscles just got a workout. It's important to work out those muscles in rehearsal rather than in front of your audience. Think about speech rehearsal as getting ready for the big game; it's a time to get mentally *and* physically prepared. If you have a hard time enunciating, or over-enunciating, try this drill.

Using Your Lips
Use this exercise to help you practice your enunciation.

Lip Drill

1. Place a pencil sideways into your mouth and bite down.

2. While holding the pencil in your mouth, rehearse your speech.

3. Now take the pencil out of your mouth

4. Repeat your speech.

- **Listen to yourself.** Recording and listening to yourself can be an uncomfortable experience, but it can go a long way to improving your diction. Listen to the recording with a copy of your speech in front of you. Make notes on words or phrases that could be clearer. Then practice those words with exaggerated articulation or the pencil trick until you feel more confident.

WILL THE AUDIENCE CARE? THINKING ABOUT TONE AND PITCH

The tone of your voice significantly impacts how your message will be received. Think about a time when a friend wanted to have a serious conversation with you. She may have said, "Can we talk?" The words "can we talk" on its own don't say very much. But if she delivered the question with a lower tone and pitch, you will begin asking yourself what you could have possibly done to upset your friend. To package our message effectively in a speech, we must consider the role of tone and pitch.

Our tone should match the occasion and goals of our speech. For example, you don't want to sound too energetic when delivering a eulogy, and you don't want to sound melancholy when delivering a toast. In the same way, the tone you take in your presentations should match the goals of your speech. Unfortunately, the tone we often hear students adopt is one of disinterest. That tone never works.

So how do you have the most engaging tone for your presentations? Varying your pitch can help create an effective tone. Delivering a line with a higher pitch can add energy to the sentence. Delivering a sentence with a lower pitch can help communicate power or seriousness. As speakers we generally want to avoid sounding monotonous. Varying your pitch to match the emotional tone of your speech's content can go a long way in strengthening your message.

You might think you have limited vocal range but, like everything else, an effective vocal range comes from practice. Even the most tonally deficient among us is capable of impressive vocal delivery and can intuitively understand how to deploy it based on the circumstance. We just have to try it out!

Exercise or Advice on Tone and Pitch

Step 1: Say the following phrases out loud. Listen to your pitch at the end of the phrase. Determine whether it went up or down and mark the appropriate box.

I hurt my finger just now.	☐ Up ☐ Down
It is hurt pretty badly.	☐ Up ☐ Down
Can you take me to the hospital?	☐ Up ☐ Down
I am really sorry that I am getting blood all over your upholstery.	☐ Up ☐ Down

Step 2: Nice work. Now say the following phrases, manipulating your pitch to match the suggested meaning.

Phrase	Meaning
Do you want to borrow my bicycle?	Like you *don't* want to lend her your bicycle.

No, that white greasepaint smeared all over your face does not make you look like a clown at all.	Like the greasepaint *does* in fact make him look clownish.
Do you really think that your pet dog ran away?	Like you actually left the front door open.
Oh yeah, I'm a huge fan of bigotry and linguistic violence.	Like you actually hate bigotry and linguistic violence.
Is your father really the King of Switzerland?	Like you don't believe that statement.

Tying It Together: Authentic Communication

With the highly complex tools of vocal production and artic-ulation, we are capable of creating a tremendous range of sounds. Opera singers know this, but many public speakers do not. In public speaking courses and seminars we've taught, students often take their vocal delivery for granted. We under-stand why people do this. They've been talking their entire lives, so why bother exercising something that's second nature. What few people realize is that speaking effectively and authen-tically requires coordination. Our posture can play a huge role in our vocal performance. Choosing when we breathe, where we gather our breath, and the way we hold our chin all play a role in how the audience receives our message. Your voice can change minds, so you need to know how to train it.

Even more than our physical bodies, our voice is a projection of ourselves; it is our ego put into action, our own ideas and thoughts laid bare to the world. We are incredibly familiar with our own voice, yet it can still be foreign to us. We only hear it from within our own heads, after all. It's always amazing (and amusing) to watch a child (or adult) hear their own recorded voice played back to them for the first time: Is that really me? Do I really sound like that?

A controlled, polished vocal performance requires something similar of us: we have to get outside of our own heads. By actively thinking about and practicing the various processes involved in vocal production, we can put this incredible instrument to better use. Ironically, we can find our voice by learning to control our voice.

LET'S ANALYZE A SPEECH (AND THEN GIVE ONE)

Now it's your turn to analyze vocal delivery.

Step 1: Below is an excerpt from John F. Kennedy's famous 1961 Inaugural Address. You can find a video of the address at http://www.jfklibrary.org/Asset-Viewer/Archives/USG-17 .aspx). This excerpt is located at 2:00–3:33 on the video. While listening to President Kennedy, try scoring the text in a way that reflects how he performed it. You can use our key and symbols from above, or you can create your own. You may need to pause and replay to keep up.

Inaugural Address (January 20, 1961), John Fitzgerald Kennedy

The world is very different now. For man holds in his mortal hands the power to abolish all forms of human poverty and all forms of human life. And yet the same revolutionary beliefs for which our forebears fought are still at issue around the globe—the belief that the rights of man come not from the generosity of the state but from the hand of God.

We dare not forget today that we are the heirs of that first revolution. Let the word go forth from this time and place, to friend and foe alike, that the torch has been passed to a new generation of Americans—born in this century, tempered by war, disciplined by a hard and bitter peace, proud of our ancient heritage—and unwilling to witness or permit the slow undoing of those human rights to which this nation has always been committed, and to which we are committed today at home and around the world.

Step 2: Now score a speech that you wrote for a previous chapter.

Key Concepts

- Effective speaking starts with effective diaphragmatic breathing.

- Sound is produced by airflow through the larynx and vocal cords; words are formed by the articulatory tools: lips, cheeks, palate, teeth, and tongue.

- Effective speakers plan their vocal delivery in advance of their speech, scoring their speech to produce maximum impact.

- Speakers must match their volume to their room and their purpose.

- Speakers must work hard to deliver their speeches at an acceptable, understandable rate.

- Variations in volume, rate, and tone can increase an audience's attention.

CHAPTER 11

Audience Analysis

Speaking in public is a partnership. The speaker expresses her thoughts; the audience, meanwhile, reacts, approving, criticizing, and questioning what she says. Speakers who ignore the audience will fail. Preparation and practice can help the speaker deliver a polished performance, but that's only part of the work needed. The speaker must deliver a polished performance that works in concert with her audience. To accomplish this, speakers must analyze and prepare to interact with their listeners. This chapter will help you do that.

What Makes Each Audience Unique

Every public-speaking event is unique; no two speakers are the same, no two speeches are same, and no two audiences are the same. Even if you are giving a speech to the same group of people you spoke to previously, the audience is still different: maybe they've changed their attitudes, maybe they're hungrier than they were earlier. Each audience is unique, and so understanding what makes them distinctive is important. When analyzing your audience examine three factors:

1. **Demographics.** What are the demographic characteristics of the audience? By demographics, we mean the basic factors that define the audience: Is the audience old or young? Male or female? Will there be people of different races among your listeners? Is your audience affluent? Demographics give you a broad sketch of your audience and can often help you adapt your material.

2. **Social location.** Consider the experiences of your audience. Are there particular reasons why members have gathered? Do they all share a profession? Was the audience invited? Did they choose to attend your speech or was it a class assignment? The professions, interests, and histories of your audience members make up their social location. These factors are often more important than demographic composition because they offer a more nuanced view of the audience's outlook.

3. **Values and beliefs.** Our cultural background, religious associations, where we live and work, and other aspects of our identities shape our values and beliefs. Our *values* are our core understandings of right and wrong that guide our attitudes and behaviors. Our *beliefs*, on the other hand, are applications of values to particular circumstances or issues. Values are typically determined by our social location and culture, and deal with broad ideals. Beliefs spring from these values, are focused on specific issues, and may represent the resolution of competing values. For example, you may come from a military family, and so you may value patriotic service; at the same time, you were raised

to value all forms of life. As a result, you may respect and value individuals in the military while not believing that every war is just. This is only one (admittedly complex) example of how values and beliefs interact.

Our beliefs may change over time and through our experiences with others, whereas our values tend to stay relatively constant. Therefore, changing an audience member's core values is extremely difficult; changing his beliefs is more reasonable. In fact, by tapping into an audience's value system, you can make changing their beliefs even easier.

FRAMES OF REFERENCE

Our background, social location, beliefs, and values all influence how we process and interpret the information we see and hear; and in turn, that information influences our messages and how we deliver them. We enter each interaction with a particular *frame of reference*. Our history, ethnicity, gender identity, sexual orientation, religious beliefs, and cultural norms all comprise our frame of reference. Each new interaction in some way influences that frame of reference. For example, you may have spent your entire life believing that green beans are disgusting. So, when you meet Jill, the green bean farmer, for the first time, you may be a bit uneasy, given your particular frame of reference. Through your interactions with Jill, you may come to love green beans or you may hate them even more. This new interaction alters your frame of reference toward green beans.

Our frame of reference is interconnected with our identity. Who we *are* is in many ways that amalgamation of our experiences and interactions. For most of us, our frame of reference is a continually evolving aspect of the self. When you encounter a message that conflicts with your frame of reference, you may initially feel that the message and the messenger are wrong. But, if the speaker presents compelling arguments, you may change your mind.

Learning About Your Audience

So now that we know what makes our audience unique and understand the importance of this information in determining the success or failure of our speech, let's discuss how you can get to know your audience. Your analysis should influence how your speech is written and delivered. Audience analysis can inform what language you may want to avoid and what may be advantageous. You can gather relevant data in many ways. If your speech takes place in a classroom setting, consider the following options:

- **Survey your audience.** Designing a short questionnaire can help you assess your audience's beliefs about your topic. All persuasive speeches involve a controversial subject matter, that is, an issue with at least two opposing sides. Consider polling your audience to determine a) if they are aware of the controversy, and b) where they currently stand on the issue. Once you have a better idea of your audience's frame of reference, you can tailor your message to target their values and improve your chances of achieving the goals of your speech.

- **Pay attention during discussion.** Another easy way to gather information about your audience's frame of reference is by listening to what they say during discussion in and around the venue. Really listen and ask questions; you'll be amazed at how much you can learn about your audience long before you speak.

- **Get to know your audience outside of the event.** Some audiences are less vocal than others. If your audience seems a bit subdued, ask them their opinions of your topic outside the event, during breaks. Their opinions may go a long way in developing strong refutations to the counterarguments in your speech. Ask follow-up questions to gain a better understanding of their frame of reference. These sorts of adaptations can be made even during a speech event. Information gathered before you speak can help you address concerns or clarify something the audience found confusing.

The preceding advice was great for those giving speeches in class, but what if you do not have access to your audience beforehand?

- **Reach out to other/past speakers.** You may be called to speak at an event where the audience is composed of complete strangers. If this is the case, contact past guest speakers. Ask them about their experience with the audience. To what aspects of the speech was the audience positively responsive? Ask if past speakers have any recommendations for subjects to avoid.

- **Do not be guided by assumptions.** While we highly suggest gathering as much information about your audience as possible, you should not be guided by assumptions. You will assume some things about your audience. Making assumptions is what we, as humans, inherently do; but no matter what you think you know about the audience, you must always be open to surprises. Let's say you're delivering a speech at the United Grandmas Convention. You decide to write a speech about knitting because, in your mind, all grandmas LOVE knitting. Then you find out that it is a Rock n' Roll Grandmas Convention and these ladies HATE knitting.

More seriously, we want to interpret the audience, not *mis-*interpret them. Through audience analysis you can make educated guesses, but you should avoid pigeonholing your audience. And never resort to stereotypes when constructing your messages.

LAST-MINUTE AUDIENCE ANALYSIS

A few minutes before you speak, take stock of the audience. This is your last opportunity to try to understand them and to confirm or dispel any assumptions you might have made about them. Your analysis of the demographics or the purpose of the audience may not change very much. For instance, if you are speaking to your class, your class is probably going to show up. What might change, though, is the emotional and mental state of the audience. Are they tired? Did they just eat? Will you be speaking to a packed house or three people each sitting in different sections of the theater? This is the time to use visual cues to determine what's going on.

IDENTIFYING A TARGET AUDIENCE

Obviously, there will be a group of people at your speaking event, but are they your *target audience,* those in your audience who you want to influence? The concept of a target audience is a fundamental component of audience analysis.

Your target audience can be determined by many factors. It may be the people you will be speaking to, but it is more likely to be some subsection of that group. If you're talking to a group of guys (or girls), but you secretly have a crush on Henry (or Henrietta), then Henry(etta) is your target audience. You are speaking to the whole group but aiming to persuade a target audience.

Many factors might define your target audience. They might be the portion of the audience that controls some important outcome for you (like a teacher or a judge, or Henrietta). They might be the portion that is more persuadable (like swing voters, your grandparents, or, hopefully, Henrietta). They might be those you think are most important to persuade (people in a position to make a difference or whose behavior you are specifically targeting). Any or all of these factors might help you focus your performance and the content of your speech.

Applying Your Audience Analysis to Your Performance

Once you've learned as much as you can about your audience, you need to apply this analysis to your performance. Knowing what the audience wants or expects can help you make important and useful changes in both the content and form of your speech.

ADAPTING CONTENT

We do not advocate radically changing your speech or viewpoint to adapt to your audience, but you can still utilize some effective strategies, based on your audience analysis, to enhance the content of your speech.

- **Capitalize on common ground to persuade effectively.** To the extent that your audience is friendly, you can use shared values and frames of reference to execute a great speech. Convincing an audience of cat lovers to donate to a local cat shelter can be pretty straightforward, but what if your audience isn't cat lovers? Connect your concerns with what they care about. What if they're teachers? Well, maybe you might use the audience's love of children as a way into their hearts; they love kids, kids love kittens—and there you have your connection.

- **Use an audience's prior knowledge to your advantage.** By identifying the areas where your audience is likely to be sympathetic to your cause, you can build a successful speech on a solid foundation. Identifying these areas also helps you determine where more or less effort will be needed to give the audience the information they need. The cat lovers in the first example probably don't need to be told why cats are great; you can therefore focus on persuading them to donate to the shelter. Speaking to a group of airline pilots about flight mechanics will necessitate a different level of background information than speaking on the same subject to a group of schoolteachers.

- **Provide counterarguments to address potential audience concerns.** If you are facing a less-than-friendly audience, you must do some additional adapting to overcome their opposition. This is where having a *counterargument* is important. A counterargument is a response you might anticipate to an argument an audience could make against your ideas. Challenging your ideas doesn't only occur in a persuasive speech; someone also might question the importance of your topic in an informative speech. If your audience analysis suggests that you might face this sort of resistance, address it head-on.

  A good counterargument begins by laying out the objection or issue you need to address. Do this in a nonpolarizing way, if possible. For example:

  > Many people object to spending taxpayer dollars on this sort of project. . .

You might be thinking, "Whoa, Jeff, that's not very funny. . ."

These examples put the audience's objections into words and allow the speaker to proceed with a reply; they do not put the audience on the defensive, like these (bad examples):

Some wacko nutjobs are worried about taxpayer dollars. . .

And if you don't think I'm funny, you can just shut up.

After you (gracefully) introduce the objection, you can proceed with a response. Ideally you will use some of the strategies mentioned above, possibly appealing to the audience's values to help change their beliefs.

ADAPTING FORM

Now that you have a good idea of what content you want to include in your speech based on your audience analysis, you need to consider how you will package that information. Your presentation's overall tone and the way of explaining information should also be informed by your knowledge of your audience and their frame of reference. In determining these factors, you have two stylistic choices to make.

- **Humor or formality.** Some audiences respond well to humor. Some audiences may find humor to be inappropriate depending on the topic or occasion. Some audiences will respond only to certain types of humor. The composition of some audiences suggests a more restrained use of humor. For example, if you are speaking to a group of older professionals, you may want to avoid that off-color joke you are planning to make in your second point. Additionally, audiences from a social location substantially different from your own may have a different sense of humor or may be offended by particular types of humor. In these cases, you may choose to keep the speech more formal.

- **Evidence or examples.** The amount of technical evidence you relay to your audience should be proportional to the amount of prior knowledge they have about the subject. A speech on 3D printing will be received differently by a class of graduating engineers than a class of 4th graders. You can reasonably assume that the engineers have prior knowledge of the technology and so you can include more technical language. For lay audiences, or audiences who are not as interested in your topic, you may need to include more examples or metaphors to make sure they understand and care about your message.

SPEAKER SPOTLIGHT

Kenneth Phillips
Artistic Director of the Possibility Project

Kenneth Phillips has used the performing arts to teach social emotional learning and youth development for over ten years. This means he gets to spend a lot of his time engaging teenagers and young adults in poetry, acting, singing, dancing, play writing, and public speaking toward goals pertaining to personal development and social change advocacy. To do his job effectively, he knows he must adapt to his audience.

Confidence, the ability to formulate clear and concise thoughts or arguments, how to listen to both verbal and nonverbal feedback, and the basic psychological self-awareness that comes with trying to understand how you are perceived by others will help you be effective in a wide variety of settings and relationships.

When asked to present at Columbia University about the work that I do, I was expecting a small panel of interested persons and a round table discussion. When I arrived I was directed to an auditorium full of teachers and students and pushed onto a stage. There were a lot of very intelligent questions from the audience after my presentation. It was an intense experience and I enjoyed it thoroughly.

I get nervous. Nervous is good. It means you are about to do something important. Preparation is the key to overcoming stage fright.

Know your audience. I will definitely change the way in which I present information based on the audience I am trying to reach. Examples of how to curtail your message in order to achieve your communicative goals can include: avoiding or integrating specific jargon or lingo, what jokes or attention-getting devices you may or may not use, what sorts of visual aides are appropriate, and choosing carefully the extent to which you utilize your vocabulary.

Playing music teaches me a lot about gauging audience response, though. It's important to be able to give the audience an experience that they enjoy. If the crowd is loud and rowdy, it's generally not a good idea to force feed them your newest love ballad. You'd need to move it around in the set list or take it out completely and be prepared to play a more appropriate song that you hadn't intended on performing that night. Being able to make adjustments and improvise in the moment can make a real difference in how well a presentation is received.

Develop a repertoire of jokes, ice breakers, attention getters, and quips that you can use when you need to. These can help bail you out of awkward moments when they arise. Also, consistently practice not using verbal filler in your day-to-day communication. As they say, "what you do off stage will show up on stage."

In the End, Everyone is a Kindergartner

Here's a hot tip. Ignore everything else in this chapter and treat all audiences as if they are composed of five-year-olds. When we talk to five-year-olds, we take time to explain difficult concepts. We also check in with them frequently to ensure that they are paying attention. We don't rush. We make funny voices to command their attention, and we don't give a flip if they think we are buffoon or not. Because they are five. And there is no way they think that we are buffoons. But here's the thing, if we make silly voices to command attention, a room full of nuclear physicists will not think that we are buffoons, either. They will think that we care about them enough to entertain them enough to risk being seen as a buffoon. They will think us brave. And most importantly, they will not think we know any less about nuclear physics. If we have done our homework, know our content, and speak with conviction, then the other stuff—the funny voices—adds to the presentation. They help us stand out. They make our message memorable to every audience.

Tying It Together: Authentic Communication

Public speaking is a two-way street. More so than many art forms, the speaker and her audience are connected by an intimate and immediate feedback loop. The planning that a speaker puts into her speech will dictate how pleasant (or unpleasant) this loop is. When perfecting your speech, make sure you do it with your audience's experience in mind.

Of course, as we said earlier, we want you to be yourself; speak your truth, and don't let a hostile audience put you off your path. Whenever possible, though, set out to meet your audience halfway. Invite them to walk your path with you for a while, and make it easier for them to do so by making them feel comfortable. Speak to their values, to their experiences, to their frame of reference. Challenge them when necessary, but welcome them when possible.

And Afterward, Go to Disney World!

Step 1: You want to go to Disney World. Prepare two arguments for why you should go. Consider how much fun you'll have, or maybe some specific attractions at the park, or maybe what you can learn there.

Step 2: Now modify your arguments (and approach) for different audiences, based on their values and possible concerns.

Audience	Values	Concerns
Parents	You, Family Fun	Cost
A School Principal	Education, Children	Safety
Best Friend	Fun, Making Memories	Leaving Becky out. . .

Step 3: Deliver your speech to one of these audiences.

Key Concepts

- Every audience is unique and deserves a uniquely tailored performance.

- An audience's demographics, social location, and value and beliefs make up their frame of reference.

- There are many ways to learn more about your audience, from surveys well in advance of a speech to a quick peek around the curtain right before a speech.

- Consider who your target audience is.

- Use audience analysis to adapt the content and the form of your speech.

- When in doubt, be entertaining and engaging enough to hold the attention of five-year-olds.

CHAPTER 12

The Speaking Experience

You've made it through eleven chapters; you've worked hard to prepare for your speech. Now the moment you will deliver your speech is close. How will you feel on speech day? What will you experience before, during, and after your speech? Maybe it will go something like this:

> You are sitting in waiting, watching the last presentation before it's your turn. You're giving the speaker all the signals to indicate that you're paying attention. You nod in agreement. You even laugh at the joke she made in her second point. Was it her second point? Wait. What's your second point? Oh no. You know what it *is*, but how did you phrase the transition? Her words begin bleeding into yours. You've practiced your presentation over and over and NOW your mind is failing you. She sounds like she's wrapping up.

Your heart is beating like crazy and you're wondering if your teacher will notice if you dig in your bag to retrieve your outline. You just want to know how you phrased the transition. If you don't recall the transition, your entire second point will go down in flames. You're spinning out of control as the audience applauds your predecessor. The master of ceremonies takes a few final notes and calls your name. You feel like your arms will fall off.

Don't worry! We can get you through this. Remember your training. You've done a speech at the end of every chapter. You eat moments like this for breakfast. And in this future hypothetical you will have already read Chapter 12: The Speaking Experience, and you will be prepared to give one heck of a speech.

Preparation is a Process

To have a good speaking experience, speakers must be adequately prepared, so it's good to construct a schedule for your preparation process. This schedule helps break down a potentially intimidating task into more manageable pieces. A successful preparation process will include five stages:

1. Conceptualization

2. Visualization

3. Completion

4. Trust

5. Delivery

The time frame for these stages may vary based on the situation, but we've included an ideal schedule below.

CONCEPTUALIZING THE SPEECH: ONE MONTH IN ADVANCE

Most public speaking events give speakers a lot of advance notice: successful speakers take advantage of this time to begin assembling their speech. Much of what occurs in this stage has been covered in earlier chapters: topic selection (Chapter 5), researching for the speech (Chapter 6), outlining the speech (Chapter 7), etc. We don't have anything to add here, but we want to reinforce the importance of preparing well in advance. The less you have to worry about the content of your speech, the more you can focus on delivering the best speech possible.

After researching and outlining your speech, you should complete your first (or first few) drafts. You definitely don't want to be memorizing while you are revising, or worrying about your wording as you try to figure out the logistics of your presentation.

VISUALIZING THE SPEECH: TWO WEEKS BEFORE

In this stage of the process, you are moving from *conceptualizing* the speech as a set of ideas on paper to *visualizing* the speech as an event that will actually take place. Around two weeks before you are scheduled to present, gather information about the logistical aspects of the presentation. Let's explore each element of this stage more fully.

- **Know your venue.** Initially, gather as much information as you can about your venue. If you are speaking in your regular classroom, take notes about the space. Are there windows in the back of the classroom that can create an annoying glare? Make a note about the acoustics of the room. If the room echoes when your teacher speaks, make note of that. If there is a loud air conditioner in the room, note that too. You may not be able to do much about some issues, but at least they won't surprise you on speech day.

If you are speaking in an unfamiliar space, email the event coordinator and ask if there are pictures of the venue available online. The more information you gather, the more comfortable you'll be on the day of the speech. We are really comfortable speaking in our living room because we know the space intimately. Knowledge of your surroundings is a great way to reach that same level of comfort.

- **Know your technology.** Examine the technology at your disposal and determine if it can enhance your presentation. For example, you may be interested in including visual aids. What technology is available to facilitate this? Even if you hadn't planned on using visual aids, the technology in the venue may inspire you to do so. Either way, it's important to know what technology is available and how it works.

  Take stock of the technology in your venue. If your venue has a projector, ask for instructions on using it. Can the projector be controlled remotely, or do you have to strike the keyboard to change slides? Does the projector have a weird tendency to turn on or off on its own? If your venue does not have this technology, how will you be able to show your physical presentation aids? Again, this process is all about gathering information so you can practice the speech efficiently and anticipate problems.

  Once you know what technology is available, design your visual aids so you can practice with them in the next stage of the preparation process.

- **Show your speech to a helpful person.** By this point, you have a speech, you know about your venue, and you have incorporated visual aids based on the technology available. Now it's time to show your speech to an actual person. All too often, students rehearse exclusively to a wall, a mirror, or a robot dog. While this can help you gain some confidence in the language of your speech, you need human contact. We do not present our speeches in front of walls; we present in front of people. So in order to master your speech, rehearse in front of real people.

  Showing your speech to a person you trust is tremendously helpful. In addition to gaining confidence, you can also receive helpful feedback about moments of your speech that are confusing or could use further clarification. Your speaking companion may have a great idea for a joke or some other "fix" that could increase your confidence.

COMPLETING THE SPEECH: ONE WEEK BEFORE

If you have planned everything according to the timeline, a week before your speech, you should feel pretty confident about the content. You have given your speech to a helpful person, who has offered constructive feedback. Now it is time to enter the last phase of your preparation.

- **Tweak your speech.** Respond to the feedback you received. Notice that we didn't say, "Incorporate all of the feedback you've received from anyone who offered it." You may, in fact, reject some of the ideas others have offered. It's important to keep in mind that, ultimately, this is *your* speech. You need to have the confidence to stand behind everything you say.

- **Rehearse.** Your speech is finished. It's beautiful! Every word has been meticulously chosen to move your audience. There will never be another speech on 3D printing technology as moving as yours. We're happy for you! Now it's time for a serious rehearsal.

  To begin the rehearsal stage, determine whether you will be delivering your speech from limited notes. If you are, create them. Students will often wait until the night before the big speech to do this. They then panic and print every single word of their speech on the cards. Preparing your notes ahead of time will help you learn your cues and increase your overall comfort with the language of your speech.

  Finally, ask a friend or family member you trust to watch your speech. Pay attention to the types of feedback they offer. Did they laugh at your attention-getting joke? If they didn't, determine why. Were they confused by the language or do you need to tweak the timing of your delivery to get the laugh? Practicing in front of a small, friendly audience will help solidify final adjustments to your delivery and boost your confidence for the big day.

TRUSTING THE SPEECH: THE NIGHT BEFORE

The first thing to do on the night before your speech is easy: nothing. Relax. Don't worry about memorization, don't think about changing anything in your text, don't practice your speech. Spending the night working on your speech will rarely produce any noticeable benefits, but will likely stress you out and degrade your performance. So relax.

Focus on the minor things. Assemble your materials: lay out your clothes, your bag, your visual aids, whatever you can do to make your day-of process less stressful. Do just a little logistical work tonight to take the stress off tomorrow.

DELIVERING THE SPEECH: THE DAY OF

Okay, now you've *really* made it. It's the day of your speech. It's go-time! We want your speech to go smoothly, so here's some important last-minute advice to help you give a great performance.

- **Say the first three words slowly.** When you are standing in front of an audience and about to speak, you're not really ready. You think you are, but even with lots of rehearsal, you are not completely certain about what sound will come out of your mouth. Nor are you certain about how the audience will react. You may have anxiety about the room and the equipment, but most likely you'll be anxious about the audience. How will they react to your speech? Will they be able to follow your arguments?

  Because all of this anxiety and thinking and analyzing is happening at once, the beginning of a speech is a critical time that will inform the speech's success. So you must focus on your audience and their needs. You, as the speaker, have the ability (and responsibility) to help the audience understand your important message, and that means starting your speech off right. How do you do it? Say the first three words slowly—way more slowly than normal. This ensures that the audience has time to process your voice and that you have time to ease into your speech. If you start fast, the audience is lost immediately and spends the next few moments playing catch-up (instead of appreciating your ideas). Speak slowly and the audience will be processing what you are saying as you say it.

- **Keep your energy up.** You need to work hard to maintain your energy throughout the speech. Using the speech-scoring method discussed in Chapter 10, be sure to include a high-energy moment or two early in your speech. We hope you have a good Attention-getting Device to get things going, but you want to overcompensate and follow up with a high-energy moment in order to maintain the audience's attention. As the speech continues, make strong, clear choices about when you will inject fresh energy into your performance; without your commitment to energy, your audience will lose interest.

Don't put your audience to sleep! Keep your energy up! Exclamation points for everyone!

- **Respond to your audience.** As you are speaking, you will find that your audience moves around quite a bit. They may laugh, they may cry, they may cough, sneeze, burp, shuffle, lean, stretch, nod, shake; they may check their phones. You need to read these reactions and react in turn. If the audience is laughing at a joke, pause and let them laugh. Maybe smile with them. If the audience seems tired or antsy, raise your energy level (or your volume).

  Don't be discouraged if some members of the audience don't pay close attention to your speech. Regardless of how brilliant you are, someone will be distracted. Instead of focusing on these distracted or disinterested audience members, seek out the best listener in the room. You know this person: they make great eye contact, they take notes, and they nod to show they understand you. Make this person your "safe space"; return to them frequently to get that little boost of confidence you need.

Kerri Hannan
United States Foreign Service Officer

Kerri's fifteen years on the job have required (and trained) her to be comfortable in a variety of different roles. Whether it be representing American foreign policy as the spokesperson at the U.S. embassy in Afghanistan or promoting cultural exchange in Argentina, communication is fundamental to her career as a diplomat. As a foreign service officer, she is required to communicate information of great importance every day, making her an expert on the speaking experience.

With a degree in zoology from the University of Florida, my first training in public speaking was giving presentations to my fellow students about my research on macaws. These audiences were curious and friendly, and helped me develop my confidence.

As a diplomat, I have to communicate American values with foreign audiences of all types, sometimes unfriendly ones, so it is critical that I be engaging and that they perceive me as open and honest.

I need to know my subject but also share it in a convincing and interesting way. This skill serves me in small meetings with colleagues and when I had only a few moments to brief the secretary of state on breaking news. Knowing to put the lead first, to summarize key information, to speak to the audience, has helped me become a stronger communicator and better at my job.

Everyday I have meetings, give presentations, or do radio and TV interviews to talk about U.S. foreign policy or programs sponsored by the U.S. embassy. Sometimes this is done in a foreign language.

I remember hearing Secretary Hillary Clinton the first day she came to the State Department [in 2009]. She stood in the entrance of the main building and told personal stories of how she believed in the value of diplomacy and the work of U.S. diplomats. She was warm and honest but also conveyed a sense of purpose, laying out her goals for the coming years. She also made us feel that she was "one of us" now. It was obvious that she took the time to think about her audience and what message she wanted them to receive, and it set the tone for her entire tenure. That day she gained a lot of genuine support from her "troops."

I try to anticipate any tough questions I will have and prepare an answer or address them in my remarks. Being clear and direct is critical, especially when sharing important information with non-native English speakers.

People remember stories and interesting facts. The story can be someone else's, but it is better if you are sharing your own experience. It will force you to think more broadly about your topic and how it relates to your own life.

Enthusiasm is contagious.

If you get a chance, speak in classrooms of younger students. They are great for practicing how to keep an audience's attention, and they will certainly let you know if you don't seem to know your topic.

RECOVERY
No matter how much time you've spent composing your speech, no matter how much you've practiced, something will go wrong. Either something will happen that you can't control, or you will make a mistake (which is inevitable). Accept this. But the beauty of public speaking is that great speakers are not defined by the inevitable hesitation (flub) or memory lapse. Great speakers are defined by their unflinching commitment

to their message. Here are a few ways to help you recover from common slip-ups.

- **Disruptions.** We've all seen it happen: A well-meaning custodian enters the room while a speaker is in the climax of her presentation and empties the trash, or a siren goes off nearby. The audience immediately becomes distracted. This is an understandably uncomfortable experience, but you have several ways of handling these types of situations. If the disruption is brief, like the custodian taking out the trash, keep talking. The less attention you pay to the disruption, the sooner the audience will return their attention to you. However, if the disruption prevents your audience from hearing your speech, pause. During this break, remember where you left off. Once the disruption has ended, simply say, "Before the break we were discussing _____." Then continue.

- **Flubs.** Brief stutters or hesitations in your speech, sometimes called "flubs," can happen to the most gifted orators. When they happen to you, avoid drawing attention to the mistake. Too often, speakers react to the flub by making a frustrated face or sound; these reactions waste energy on the flub and enhance the audience's awareness of the mistake. Don't put more energy into your flubs. If they happen, pretend they didn't, breathe, and move on.

- **Memory lapses.** Forgetting your lines usually happens only when you let anxiety take control. In many instances, students will begin apologizing when this happens, saying things like, "I'm sorry" or "I lost my place." What these students fail to realize is that apologizing wastes valuable cognitive energy. Essentially, your brain is thinking about the apology and *not* the next line of your speech!

When you have a lapse, keep in mind that the heart of your message matters more than what you've written word-for-word. If you've lost your place in your speech, simply take a moment to breathe and collect your thoughts. More than likely, the next line of your speech will come to you.

CONFIDENCE: FAKE IT UNTIL YOU MAKE IT

A lot of this advice comes back to one, central attribute: confidence. So here's the last piece of advice. No one knows what's going through your mind when you are on stage. Maybe you missed a word; maybe you mixed up the order of your arguments. Whatever the case, the audience only knows what you reveal. Using the techniques taught throughout this book, you will be able to keep cool under pressure and keep pushing forward. If you project confidence, the audience will perceive you as confident. Eventually, your feelings will align with their perception: each successful speech, each successful moment of each speech, will improve your confidence.

Tying It Together: Authentic Communication

The most important, and unfortunately intangible, attribute that can make or break a speech is the notion of "being present." You came to this speech with an idea to express, and your process of preparation has refined and improved that idea as much as possible. Speech day is a time to enjoy the moment and to reflect on your own performance. Remember that each speaking experience is an opportunity not just to impress but also to learn and improve. You can move forward only by being present in the moment and recognizing areas for improvement.

Relax. You're going to do a great job.

Practicing Dealing With Disruptions

Using a prepared speech (and a friend to simulate the distractions), plan and practice how you will respond to each of the following potential disruptions.

1. The audience laughs extra hard at one of your jokes.

2. An ambulance rolls by as you are mid-sentence.

3. You forget what sentence is next (have your friend simulate this by poking you hard in the ribs).

4. A baby starts crying as you begin your first main idea.

5. A cell phone goes off.

6. A tiger gets loose in the audience.

Key Concepts

- The preparation process has five steps: conceptualization, visualization, completion, trust, and delivery.

- In the conceptual stage, you will research and outline your speech and complete a first draft.

- Use the visualization stage to familiarize yourself with your venue, your technology, and your visual aids.

- In the completion stage, you will make final changes to your speech and rehearse.

- Trust your speech. The night before, try to relax and make your speech day easier and less stressful.

- Say the first three words of your speech very slowly to let the audience acclimate themselves to your voice.

- Keep your energy and confidence levels high throughout your speech, even if you stumble.

Endnotes

Chapter 1: Introduction to Public Speaking

1. Glenn Croston, "The Thing We Fear More Than Death," *Psychology Today* (November 29, 2012). https://www.psychologytoday.com/blog/the-real-story-risk/201211/the-thing-we-fear-more-death.

Chapter 2: Theory of Public Speaking

1. Michael Maxwell, "World History Timeline: 4 Eras of History," *World History Timeline: 4 Eras of History*. 1 Jan. 2011.

2. Battiscombe Gunn, *The Instruction of Ptah-Hotep*, (London: John Murray, 1906).

3. Peter DeCaro, "The Origins of Public Speaking," *www.publicspeakingproject.org.* 5 Feb. 2015.

4. "General Summary of Aristotle's Appeals: Ethos, Pathos, and Logos." http://courses.durhamtech.edu/perkins/aris.html.

5. Quintilian, *Institutio Oratoria,* http://penelope.uchicago.edu/Thayer/E/Roman/Texts/Quintilian/Institutio_Oratoria/home.html.

6. The Bedford Bibliography for Teachers of Writing: A Brief History of Rhetoric and Composition. http://bedfordstmartins.com/Catalog/static/bsm/bb/history.html.

Chapter 3: Overcoming Communication Apprehension

1. Nick Morgan, "My Most Embarrassing Public Speaking Moment," Forbes (Dec. 7, 2011). http://www.forbes.com/sites/nickmorgan/2011/12/07/embarrassed-about-being-embarrassed-dont-be-embrace-your-humanity/.

2. D. R. Godden, and A. D. Baddeley, "Context Dependent Memory in Two Natural Environments: on Land and Underwater," British Journal of Psychology 66, no. 3 (1975). http://onlinelibrary.wiley.com/doi/10.1111/j.2044-8295.1975.tb01468.x/abstract.

3. Fergus Craik and Robert Lockhart, "Levels of Processing: A Framework for Memory Research," *Journal of Verbal Learning and Verbal Behavior* 11, no. 6 (December 1972). http://www.sciencedirect.com/science/article/pii/S002253717280001X.

Chapter 4: Writing for the Listening Audience

1. "Many English Speakers Cannot Understand Basic Grammar," *ScienceDaily*, July 6, 2010. http://www.sciencedaily.com/releases/2010/07/100706082156.htm.

2. James Hartley, and Ivor Davies, "Note Taking: A Critical Review," *Innovations in Education and Training International* 15, no. 3 (1978): 207–224.

3. John R. Anderson, *Cognitive Psychology and Its Implications*. (New York: Freeman, 1990).

4. Courtesy Benjamin Robin, director of Individual Events and national championship public speaking coach at Western Kentucky University.

Chapter 5: Topic Selection

1. Tammy Miller, "How to: Speech Topics Are Everywhere." *Toastmaster* (February 1, 2011). http://magazines.toastmasters.org/article/How To: Speech Topics Are Everywhere/751613/72199/article.html.

2. "What Makes a Story Newsworthy," MediaCollege.com. http://www.mediacollege.com/journalism/news/newsworthy.html.

Chapter 6: Research

1. The OWL at Purdue, "Avoiding Plagiarism: Overview," *Online Writing Lab.* http://owl.english.purdue.edu/owl/resource/589/01/.

Chapter 7: Organization

1. Dana R. Carney, Amy J.C. Cuddy, and Andy J. Yap, "Power Posing: Brief Nonverbal Displays Affect Neuroendocrine Levels and Risk Tolerance," *Psychological Science OnlineFirst* September 21, 2010. http://changingminds.org/techniques/general/overall/monroe_sequence.htm.

Chapter 8: Introductions and Conclusions

1. Courtesy Noah Whinston, an American speech and debate champion, from his speech at the 2012 NSDA National Championship.

Chapter 9: Physical Delivery

1. Lauren Ann Petitto and others, "Baby Hands That Move to the Rhythm of Language: Hearing Babies Acquiring Sign Languages Babble Silently on the Hands." *Cognition* 9 (2004): 43–73.

2. Amy J.C. Cuddy, "Your Body Language Shapes Who You Are," TEDGlobal 2012 (June 2012). http://www.ted.com/talks/amy_cuddy_your_body_language_shapes_who_you_are?language=en

3. Ibid.

4. Dana R. Carney, Amy J.C. Cuddy, and Andy J. Yap. "Power Posing: Brief Nonverbal Displays Affect Neuroendocrine Levels and Risk Tolerance," *Psychological Science OnlineFirst* (September 21, 2010). http://www.people.hbs.edu/acuddy/in%20press,%20carney,%20cuddy,%20&%20yap,%20psych%20science.pdf.

5. Edward T. Hall, "A System for the Notation of Proxemic Behavior," *American Anthropologist* 65, 5 (October 1963): 1003–1026.